'The Misfit Soldier'
Edward Casey's War Story, 1914–1918

Edited by

Joanna Bourke

CORK UNIVERSITY PRESS

First published in 1999 by
Cork University Press
Cork
Ireland

© Cork University Press 1999

British Library Cataloguing in Publication Data

A CIP catalogue record for this book is available from the British Library.

ISBN 1 85918 188 0

Typesetting by Red Barn Publishing, Skeagh, Skibbereen

Printed in Ireland by ColourBooks, Baldoyle, Co. Dublin

M 104, 905/920 CAS
£8.95

'The Misfit Soldier'

Edward Casey's War Story, 1914–1918

IRISH NARRATIVES

IRISH NARRATIVES

Series edited by David Fitzpatrick

Personal narratives of past lives are essential for understanding any field of history. They provide unrivalled insight into the day-to-day consequences of political, social, economic or cultural relationships. Memoirs, diaries and personal letters, whether by public figures or obscure witnesses of historical events, will often captivate the general reader as well as engrossing the specialist. Yet the vast majority of such narratives are preserved only among the manuscripts or rarities in libraries and archives scattered over the globe. The aim of this series of brief yet scholarly editions is to make available a wide range of narratives concerning Ireland and the Irish over the last four centuries. All documents, or sets of documents, are edited and introduced by specialist scholars, who guide the reader through the world in which the text was created. The chosen texts are faithfully transcribed, the biographical and local background explored, and the documents set in historical context. This series will prove invaluable for university and school teachers, providing superb material for essays and textual analysis in class. Above all, it offers a novel opportunity for readers interested in Irish history to discover fresh and exciting sources of personal testimony.

Other titles in the series:

Andrew Bryson's Ordeal: An Epilogue to the 1798 Rebellion, edited by Michael Durey
Henry Stratford Persse's Letters from Galway to America, 1821–1832, edited by James L. Pethica and James C. Roy
A Redemptorist Missionary in Ireland, 1851–1854: Memoirs by Joseph Prost, translated and edited by Emmet Larkin and Herman Freudenberger
Frank Henderson's Easter Rising, edited by Michael Hopkinson
A Patriot Priest: The Life of Father James Coigly, 1761–1798, edited by Dáire Keogh
The Rebel in his Family: Selected Papers of William Smith O'Brien, edited by Richard and Marianne Davis
'My Darling Danny': Letters from Mary O'Connell to her son Daniel, 1830–1832, edited by Erin I. Bishop
A Policeman's Ireland: Recollections of Samuel Waters, RIC, edited by Stephen Ball
'The Misfit Soldier': Edward Casey's War Story, 1914–1918, edited by Joanna Bourke

Forthcoming titles:

Alfred Webb: The Autobiography of a Quaker Nationalist, edited by Marie-Louise Legg

David Fitzpatrick teaches history at Trinity College, Dublin. His books include *Politics and Irish Life, 1913–1921* (1977, reissued 1998) and *Oceans of Consolation: Personal Accounts of Irish Migration to Australia* (1995).

Contents

Introduction

'Daddy, what did you do in the Great War?'
'Nothing', I growled, 'You just go on and polish those medals.'

With these words, a 'misfit soldier' concludes his account of the war of
1914–18. It is a strange story, sometimes told in the meek and halting
tones of a man unsure of whether he is being sufficiently 'literary' and
at other times recited with the furious and bitter humour of a working-
class man striking a blow against the 'toffs' and 'sirs' who oppress him.
This self-designated 'misfit soldier' insists that he has not written an
autobiography — 'only famous and wealthy well-educated people
write such books', he believes. Instead he wants his memoir to be
thought of as a 'documentary enterprise, with a lot of fact, and a little
dash of fiction'. The 'fiction' is there from the start. For instance, the
author is not 'John William Roworth' (as he inscribed under the title)
but Edward Casey. We do not know why he prefers to be known as
Roworth, but he clearly is not attempting to fool his readers. After all,
by the end of the second page of his typescript he has forgotten his
pseudonym and reveals his real name. Armed with his name, we can
independently check the facts given in this memoir. Most of the details
turn out to be correct (or nearly so). In his reminiscences, he tells the
recruiting sergeant that he was born on 9 October. However, his birth
certificate states that he was born on 12 November, and his school
records give his date of birth as 28 October. All three sources agree on
the year: 1898. His mother was Ellen Casey, *née* Collins, and his father,
Joseph Casey, was a stoker at a gasworks. Both the memoir and the
school records agree that Casey attended the infants' department and
then the boys' school of St Margaret's School on the Barking Road in
Canning Town, London, until 1912, when he was fourteen years old.
The 'cause of leaving' was registered as simply 'age limit'. According
to the school records, he had at least two older siblings (both sisters,
ten and eight years older than him) and two younger siblings (a brother
and a sister born five and eight years, respectively, after him). In his

memoir he mentions two older brothers who had emigrated to Australia, but perhaps he had merely changed the sex of his two sisters.

Casey was not exaggerating the trials of living in 'the cold hard world of east London'. Kerry Street was a notoriously dirty refuge for the Irish Catholic poor. The caustic tone of Sir Walter Besant (writing at the time when Casey roamed these streets as a child) was typical of middle-class opinion about this area. Besant observed that the people of Canning Town were

> of a poor class as a rule, the children dirty and the houses small and squalid, with filthy streets, large flaring public-houses, and little shops. A music-hall provides entertainment for some, but the very frequent public-house is the chief centre for passing idle time.[1]

For Casey, though, the simple familiarities of home life, gin palaces, and the ale and porter served at the 'Lilyput' Arms are remembered warmly. His fond description of his mother frying 'bloaters' (smoked herring) on the fire on the day before he left home, and the way he recalls how 'mellow' his father was that evening when they drank 'mum's favourite drink' (black porter) to wish him luck in the army, are poignant reminders of the simple pleasures grasped by London's poor.

Despite these ties, Casey admits that the army held many attractions for boys like himself. When he walked into the army recruiting office, he was a 'very skinny, pigeon chested, hollowed cheeked, sallowed complexioned' sixteen-year-old boy pretending to be two years older. Unemployment and the prospect of a drab future were certainly factors propelling him into the armed forces, but so too was the search for excitement and his admiration of the virile strength and gaudy uniforms of Regular soldiers. Enlistment with the Royal Dublin Fusiliers seemed appropriate for a Roman Catholic with an Irish name, and Casey's father had been proud of the choice. It was a 'bloody good regiment' for any son of Irish émigrés, his father told him. And so it was that Casey found himself on the way to Victoria Barracks, Cork, with a group of Irishmen who had signed up (like Casey) in London.

His military problems began immediately. From the start there was tension between this Cockney with Irish parents and the native-born Irishmen in his regiment. The first Royal Dublin Fusiliers he met teased him about being a 'low-down bloody London Cockney' parading himself in a 'famous *Irish* regiment'. Only after Casey revealed that he had Irish relatives in Kilmallock (County Limerick) did his comrades start regarding him as 'one of them and no longer an invader'. Yet when he visited these relatives in Kilmallock and his cousin called him a 'full-blooded Irish man, born in the wrong place', Casey responded angrily. 'I ain't no Irishman', he shouts. 'I am a full-blooded Cockney, born in Canning Town a mile or so from the Bow bells, and in the biggest City in the whole bleeding world.' Although the community within which Casey was bought up was partly Irish and his mother spoke with an Irish accent, Casey belonged more to the 'community of the underclass' than to any community of Irish emigrants. Along with other families in the East End of London, he shared the uncertainties and difficulties of a life of child employment, low wages and economic deprivation. It is this perspective which enables him to sneer light-heartedly at the 'toffs' with their 'tony' accents and eye-glasses and to contrast the tall, muscular professional soldiers with the scrawny slum-dwellers. He also observes the impact of the war upon his community. With the declaration of war, Casey's father suddenly found that manual labour was in demand, and that overtime was available, and the 15s allowance sent to his mother was an immense boon to the family. Even Casey's body 'fills out' as a result of regular feeding in the army.

There was a price to pay for the beneficial effect of war on the poor. Casey had to endure military training with the 2nd Battalion of the Royal Dublin Fusiliers (48th Brigade, 16th Division) and (according to the Roll of Medals) disembarked in France on 14 December 1915. He served with the 7th and 8th Battalions in the Ypres sector and in Salonika. Service in Salonika was reserved for a relatively small proportion of British servicemen. In 1918 the British army on the Western Front numbered 1,764,000, compared with 648,000 in Italy, the Dardanelles, Salonika, Mesopotamia, Egypt, East Africa, Afghanistan,

North Russia and Vladivostok. Casey hated France as much as Salonika. The rats, lice and filth disgusted him. There was also the fear of mutilation or death. Around 7 per cent of the male population between the ages of fifteen and forty-nine were killed in the Great War. Casey was plagued with fears of annihilation. 'Will I survive? What can I do to get out of all this?', he wonders. There was a fate worse than death, though, and that was gross mutilation. In the first year of the war 17 per cent of soldiers in the 'other ranks' were wounded, a percentage that never dropped below 12 per cent during any year of the war. All parts of the body were at risk: head, shoulder, arm, chest, intestines, buttock, penis, leg, foot. While most soldiers (like Casey) longed for a 'blighty', the fear of severe injuries tormented combatants.

Casey also could not endure military discipline and engaged in a constant struggle against the rules. Like many other working-class men in both military and civilian life, he passionately resented class hierarchies that condemned him and his mates to a dangerous, dirty and hellish existence while their so-called superiors lived in comfort and took all the credit. Casey resisted; he was insubordinate. In his own mind, his repeated battles with his superior officers are legendary. At the same time, he knows that he is no hero and is not afraid to admit that he is terrified during combat. Like 40,000 other British soldiers in the first year of war, he even attempted desertion (for which he was severely punished a few times).[2] It is interesting to hear about the response of other privates to his fleeing from battle. They joke about cowardice, seem to share his contempt for exaggerated bravery, and are indulgent towards each other's faults.

Casey also suffered 'shell-shock'. At this time the medical understanding of war neuroses was a contentious one. A large proportion of medical officers insisted that these sufferers were actually malingering — that they were cowards. Indeed, many were — even Casey freely admits to attempting to avoid service by feigning madness. In 'real' cases of shell-shock, there were debates about its cause. In the early years of the war shell-shock was believed to be an organic illness caused by the violent concussion of a nearby exploding shell that paralysed the *nervi nervorum*. By the middle of the war psychological arguments had gained sway as it was recognised that emotional disturbance was sufficient cause for the symptoms. There was also considerable uncertainty about what would be the most effective cure for shell-shock. Some doctors employed painful electrical currents to the malfunctioning parts of men's bodies; others emphasised the need for discipline and devised harsh techniques aimed at developing the 'will power' of sufferers. Casey, however, was lucky. His doctors placed their faith in regimes involving rest, physiotherapy and hypnosis. Indeed, the doctors and nurse who cared for Casey were sympathetic men and women, dedicated as much to healing as to sending their patients back to the killing fields.[3]

The war is not described in wholly negative terms. There are three redeeming features: sex, comradeship, and tourism. Whether he calls it 'dipping his wick', having a 'blow thru', or getting 'grummet', sex both fascinates and frightens Casey. In the early months of the war Casey romanticises women. On the hill above Holyhead he cuddles and kisses a modest woman who attempts to explain to him what the word 'virgin' means. The Irish colleens with whom he 'walks out' are portrayed as pure maidens, unwilling even to ride their bicycle in front of him lest the sight of their ankles incite lurid thoughts. In contrast to these saints, the sinners in French brothels shock him. He describes the seductive way prostitutes sit on his lap and kiss him, but admits that on his first visit he could not maintain an erection and was thrown out (or 'given the bums' rush') when he demanded his money back, and, on the second visit, he ejaculated so quickly that it was barely pleasurable. As the war progresses, however, Casey's attitude changes. Some 'women of joy' are found to possess hearts of gold: they laugh at his jokes, give him money, and are portrayed as hapless victims of poverty (like Casey). One such prostitute, Kathy, is an Irishwoman from Kerry who insists that she is working in London 'not to help the English with their War, but to make money'. He calls her his 'lovely of the night'. Casey did not only have contact with prostitutes. He frequently mentions meeting homosexuals (he calls them 'queers' or 'queens') who offer him money to make love to them. Casey admits to taking their money, but says nothing about what he may (or may not) have offered in exchange. His reminiscences include a huge variety of sexual encounters, some of which are abundantly affectionate.

His male comrades, particularly those from Ireland, also fascinated Casey. Nearly 60,000 Irishmen were mobilised at the outbreak of hostilities (and before the conflict was over, more than 200,000 Irishmen had fought), but many of these Irish recruits did not regard themselves as fighting for Britain. As Casey attests, they 'hated the English govt.' but 'did not like the Germans' either. At the time he joined, the Royal Dublin Fusiliers were dominated by Irishmen and Catholics. However, the application of conscription to Britain (though, because of extreme political hostility, not to Ireland) rapidly led to the dilution of Irishmen in the Royal Dublin Fusiliers. In this process of 'dilution', Casey increasingly identifies himself as 'Irish' or, in his more sober moments, 'Cockney Irish'.

For Casey, the war provided an opportunity to travel. His descriptions of France, Salonika, Malta and Grimsby are evocative, but most fascinating are his detailed descriptions of life in Ireland in the early years of the war and during the Easter Rising. Through the eyes and ears of this Cockney soldier, we are given an idiosyncratic view of Irish politics. The political story is told largely through the words of other people: in particular, through the words of his cousins and his girlfriend, Agnes. His female cousin is the most radical of all, and his male cousin 'Shamas', i.e. Séamus, is a Volunteer officer in the town of Kilmallock. As he states, this was a strong republican area, and Casey is welcomed only on the grounds that 'blood is thicker than water'. His cousin points out the Royal Irish Constabulary barracks to him. This barrack was the site of an unsuccessful Fenian attack during the rising of 1867 and of a successful IRA attack in May 1920. The history of the War of Independence in Limerick explained that the destruction of Kilmallock barracks was

> an important blow against the morale and effectiveness of the local
> Royal Irish Constabulary, who regarded their barracks as impregnable; who boasted that in the days of the Fenians and Land Leaguers

> it overawed the people, and that it would continue to keep the
> unruly and seditious in their proper place in 1920.[4]

Shamas provides Casey with a potted nationalist interpretation of Irish
history. It is a story in which English representatives force Irishmen and
women to choose between starvation and emigration but whose power
to wield brute force is coming to an end. Later on in the reminiscences
Casey has the opportunity to witness at first hand the power of their
political resistance when his unit is recalled to Ireland to help crush the
Easter Rising. The tragic (and farcical) story of this republican uprising
between 24 April and 1 May 1916 is told very simply by Casey. As is
evident throughout his book, he is fundamentally interested in the fate
of the 'little people'. In his account of the rising, therefore, he devotes
as much space to the frightened squeals of an elderly woman whom he
shelters inside a urinal (her cries of 'Oh Jesus, Mary and Joseph!'
remind him of his mother) as he does to the battle raging outside.

Casey's girlfriend, Agnes, exemplifies the other side of Sinn Féin.
She was persecuted for 'walking out' with Casey (as the representative
of the 'English garrison' in Ireland). Her long raven hair was shaved,
and she was threatened with violence. Eventually she was forced to flee
to live with her sister in Liverpool, writing to Casey:

> I did not think that bigotry was so prevalent in my native land. It
> is very fashionable to hate the English, especially the Soldiers —
> saying they were invaders. [They make] no comment on the very
> large numbers of Irishmen who took the King's shilling and proved
> they were ready and willing to give their lives for their Country.
> (pp. 24–25 below)

Here, emigration is portrayed not only as an escape from poverty, but
also as a way to flee from political repression — republican in this
instance.

In addition to these explicitly political tales, Casey observes the Irish
people from the seat of his bicycle. While in training in Cork during the
first year of the war, he cycles around the countryside, stopping to

drink milk and share simple food with the local people. Casey's memory of being welcomed by Irish crowds is not faulty. It is repeated in
most memoirs concerned with these early years of the war. For
instance, Reginald G. J. Ford of the Royal Dublin Fusiliers described
leaving Ireland in 1915 as 'memorable'. He wrote:

> We shall never forget the enormous crowds assembled to bid us
> Goodbye. In places the crowds were so dense that we could not keep
> our ranks. The great bursts of cheering that greeted us from time to
> time as we marched with fixed bayonets through the city, were
> inspiring.[5]

There is a great contrast between such friendly responses in 1914–15
and the later hostile reception. During Casey's last visit to Ireland he
was advised to stay in barracks for his own safety. According to a local
priest, 'the Rebels' were 'few in numbers' but 'strong in persuasion'
and had forbidden people to socialise with soldiers. Casey's observa-
tion of the changing attitude towards soldiers in British regiments after
the Easter Rising has become a central part of the story of Irish history,
with most accounts making similar observations. For instance, Captain
J. Lowe was on leave in Dublin during the Rising. When he left for
France in May 1916, he noted:

> It was a lovely sunny day and I went for a last walk through the
> streets of Dublin. I had not gone far when I met a group of Irish
> women. Three of them immediately linked arms so I had to step off
> the pavement to make room for them. They looked me straight in
> the face with the most venemous [sic] hatred in their eyes and all
> three spat on the ground. I was glad when I started my journey to
> France.[6]

In contrast, Casey left Ireland with sadness, regretting the loss of
friendliness between Irish and English men and women and in trepida-
tion of what lay ahead.

Casey's military adventures and sacrifices are told with humour
which — perhaps — was absent at the time. The Roll of Medals shows

that he was awarded the 1914–15 Star on 17 November 1919 and both the Victory Medal and the British War Medal on 28 January 1921.[7] At the end of his memoir he emigrates to New Zealand to start a new life. We know nothing about that life except that he married and, at the age of eighty-two, wanted to leave this account for his grandchildren and other readers. This, then, is an attempt to bring the words of one Cockney Irishman to life. Casey dreamed of its publication and imagined its reception. The badge of the Royal Dublin Fusiliers is inscribed with the words 'Spectamur Agendo' ('We Are Known for Our Deeds'): in recounting his own deeds while a member of the regiment, Edward Casey judged himself to be a 'misfit soldier'.

Editorial Note

Casey's typescript is held by the Imperial War Museum at the call number 80/40/1. It was a difficult typescript to edit. The charm of the typescript is due, in large part, to his evocative style: nights are 'as dark as the inside of a cow', he says; and for the unemployed Casey wandering the streets, the London fogs are 'as cold as a Stepmother's breath and as cold as a Mother-in-law's heart'. Approximately half of his reminiscences have been omitted, including more detailed descriptions of military training, his numerous misdemeanours, and his service in Salonika. It is hoped that interested readers will seek out the original typescript.

It has been necessary to edit the account for the sake of clarity. The most noticeable feature of Casey's style is his alteration between first- and third-person pronouns. Sometimes the shift from 'I' to 'he' occurs within the space of the same sentence, as, for example, when he writes: 'during his meanderings, I would be approached by one of the Girls'. I have retained Casey's pronouns, despite the occasional confusion which this may cause. Furthermore, Casey rarely punctuates correctly. He places a comma where there should be a full stop, never uses inverted commas to indicate direct speech, and frequently fails to punctuate his story altogether or to use paragraphs. Capitalisation is generally omitted, except when indicating respect (for instance, he almost always capitalises the first letter in the words Soldier, Mother and Girl). He often spells words as he pronounces them: thus he writes 'shop winders' instead of 'shop windows' and (when quoting a Welsh woman) writes 'rarlly' instead of 'really'. In these cases I have kept the original spelling; wherever this might give rise to obscurity, I have added the correct spelling in italic type within square brackets. In other cases (such as 'sayin' instead of 'saying' and 'nave' instead of 'navy'), I have silently corrected the spelling. Practically every line of the script contains typing errors and misspellings; it would be extremely difficult for readers to make sense of what Casey is saying without correcting these errors. For the same reason, I have supplied inverted commas in all instances of direct speech. More crucially, many sentences do not make sense without the addition of other words; I have added these words in roman type within square brackets. Similarly, a number of obscure expressions are clarified within square brackets. Minor elisions are denoted by the device of three points within square brackets.

John William Roworth
[Edward Casey]

The Misfit Soldier
A War Story, 1914–1918

[Imperial War Museum, 80/40/1]

Our Soldier was a very skinny, pigeon chested, hollowed cheeked, sallowed complexioned [man], dressed in ragged reached me downs, and torn cuffs, and wearing a Cockney cloth cap, known in the area as 'sixpenorth of peak and a apporthoof cap'.[1] The cap was the only head gear worn by Dockers, shipworkers and other members of the younger working-class lads in the Canning Town area. This poverty stricken parish, part of the West Ham Borough, also included the railway stations of Tidal Basin, Custom House and Silvertown. It was on the Great Eastern Railway branch line from Fenchurch St. Station to North Woolwich whe[re] a free ferry ran across the river Thames to South Woolwich, in the County of Kent.

Being a little over 16, with a very low standard of learning, his almer mater was St. Margaret's Catholic School on the Barking Road. I[2] hated school, and was the bane of my Headmaster and the Teacher who had a very heavy hand with the cane. My Headmaster was a little man and [was] always addressed as 'Sir', and (being a staunch Catholic) was very insistent that we go to Mass on Sundays. He need not worry: my old Dad made us go to the 10 o'clock mass. Rain, hail, winter and summer, me and my seven brothers and sisters walked the two miles to the Church. Our Parish Priest, Father Malarkey, was a very bad-tempered old Man.[3] He taught us the Hail Marys, Our Father, etc. He always came at noon every school day to say the Angelus,[4] and I got many a cut with the cane across my shiny little bum. I was the standing joke of the school, being about four years in standard one, but after a big effort (and lots of cane) I managed to get up to Standard 4. I only attended about two days a week, and I love to play truant. My greatest thrill was singing in trains [and] outside the pubs, [and] being told I was the littlest and the skinniest busker in the district. At the age of 14, and to the great relief of my Teachers, [I left school]. My Parish Priest was very caustic re. my future, saying 'Casey, if you do no better at jobs than you did at this school, then God help you, my Son. I have done my best, and if I don't see you at Mass, or coming to confession, I will come to 26, Kerry [Street] and drag you by the ears to church. I'll be having a word with your Father. How a God-fearing Man like him fathered a scamp like you will always be beyond my comprehension. God bless and go with you, my Son.'

In the cold hard world of east London, and finding it hard to get work even at a bob a week, nobody wanted me, and so the years rolled on.

It was November 1914, the fogs had started and it was as cold as a Stepmother's breath and as cold as a Mother-in-law's heart. [I was] walking along the Barking Road and almost opposite my old School (which was next to a Gin Palace named the Royal Oak) was an Army recruiting office.

I had left home which was a downstairs half of about 100 slum houses in Kerry St. Somebody told me the street and about 2000 houses like ours belong to some duke or other. The only Duke I know was the name of some Pub, called the Duke's Head. [I was] one of 16 kids but only seven had survived the poverty of our slum. My old Dad was a stoker at that Beeton [*Beckton*] Gas works. Pay: one pound a week, and about 2 pound ten in the winter. So like dozens of my mates, we were hungry and thinly clad.

And now back to the Army Recruiting Office in Barking Road. The cold sleety wind swept down the river from the Arctic, chilling all and sundry. Most kids [were] going to school with no boots to wear on the icy pavements, but when you are nearly 17, well, you had to wear boots, and instead of socks Mum made us toe rags from old clothes. The area was in the throes of war fever, with all and sundry hating old Kaiser Bill and his soppy Crown Prince (his eldest Boy).[5] Posters were everywhere — on hoardings, trams, buses, railway stations, pubs, shop winders — and no matter where you looked this large poster of Lord Kitchener[6] looking right into your face, pointing his finger, saying 'your King and Country need you.' I was told he was a Field Marshall and a Hero from fighting the Savages in the strange countries far across the seas.

So our dilapidated and big-eyed Urchin, with his long hair sticking out from under his over-sized cap, stood gazing in the shop that had been rented by the British Army. A very big Soldier in a red jacket and three gold strips on both arms, and a red sash over his shoulder, was appealing to all and sundry to come in[to] the shop and join the Army. This Soldier was bigger than a copper. Down the road a little way was the Navy Recruiting Office with a sailor with bell-bottom pants, three gold stripes and cross anchors on each arm, [...] appealing to the crowd to join the Navy. He was not doing much business, but keen competition was observed in both shops, but the Army was winning hands down.

There was a very well-dressed man (he was a proper Toff) and was waiting his turn to enlist. I went up to him and asked, 'Do you fink they will let me join the Army?' This bloke looked down at me, and with a big grin said very kindly, 'No Son, [you are] too thin and well under-nourished. Its only your over-sized boots that stops you from falling through the bars of the drains. You are not military material.'

'You cheeky sod', I thought. Him saying I was not yet 18 yrs old! (that was the age they take you). So I went up to this big Sgt. [*Sergeant*], sticking out my chest about two inches bigger, [and] standing at attention, said in a very confident voice: 'I want to join the Army, and go and fight the bloody Germans.' He looked down at me. I looked up at him. He was so tall. I thought to myself: 'Blime, I wonder if its cold up there.' Smiling at me, he said in a very deep voice, 'If you are over the age of 18, can read and write, successfully pass the very strict medical examination, if your eye-sight and hearing is a very high standard, [then] His Majesty King George the fifth, The Commander of all the British Army, The Royal Navy, Emperor of India, Commander of all his Colonial Forces all around the world, the sun never sets on his Empire [will accept you].'

'Gor Blime,' I thought, 'what a mouthful!' I felt like telling him the only Empire I knew was the Musical Hall at the top of the Marsh, where for tuppence you could see the best talent in London, and if the King's Empire is no bigger than the musical hall it [is] not much cop.

I stepped inside the shop. There was a long table. Seated [at it] were four blokes all wearing collars and ties, writing and asking questions to blokes on the other side of the table. When it came to my turn to sit, this elderly bloke [...] (Christ, he talked very tony [posh], you know, like he had a plum in his mouth. Another funny thing, this old man wore eye glasses and only the upper-class wore eye glasses.) [...] [He was] looking me over and dipping his pen in the ink well, which he had to share with his mate. He had a long printed form, and he started on questions:

'Name?' 'Edward Casey.'

'Age?' '18.'

'When?' 'Last month October, 9th.'

It was lucky he did not ask me the year I was born, I would have been property stonkered: I did not know the year.

'Occupation?'

That made me ponder. First, what was 'occupation'? He helped by saying, 'Where do you work?' Thinking fast, I mumbled, 'At various jobs, at the greengrocer, at the coalman's yard.' He said, 'All right, I will put you down as a Labourer.' That suited me. I was over the first hurdle. I did not tell him I was an entertainer, sing[ing] in trains and outside pubs, and [at] Music Halls selling matches, which you bought wholesale at a penny a dozen and sold at two a penny in the pubs. Sometimes I made as much a sixpence a night. Should he tell [the bloke about] the stuff I pinched off the stall in Rathbone St. on Sundays? No, I kept all this stuff to myself. In the spur of the moment, he said, 'My real trade is a Waiter.' The bloke wrote all this down on the form. [Afterwards], thinking about what he had told the Clerk, he mused to himself: 'What is a waiter? I think it is a bloke that waits outside some factory waiting for a job.' He could say he was a business man, but did not know what a businessman did. Next question:

'Religion?' 'Retired Christian.'

The bloke, looking quite startled, [said] 'Retired Christian? Never heard of it, and you look far to young to be retired.' It means of course I'm a Roman Catholic. When I was asked, 'What are you doing now?' [I] replied, 'Resting. In other words, out of work.' [The officer said] 'Thanks Son. That is all I want from you. Go into the other room for medical examination.'

When he got in the other room, there were three posh-looking men who wore white coats, and three Soldiers with brass flashings, [and the] highly polished [letters] RAMC on their shoulders. I learnt it meant 'Royal Army Medical Corps'. Gor Blime, what a mouthful. One of them handed me a glass, vase, and told me to 'make water'. When I looked at him, he said, 'Piddle'. [I said] 'Why don't you say what you mean? Where I live the tarts and blokes say "I'm going for a piss". Make water! Never heard of it. "Piddle!"'.' One of the White Coats called me over and said, 'Strip.' They [were] the Doctors, and they all talked like all toffs, with a plum in their mouths. I noticed all the other men were taking their clothes off, so I followed suit. [All the time I was] thinking: 'These people had funny sayings. Strip. Mum always roared at us, yelling "Take those bloody clothes [off] and get to bed"!'

The [man in the] white coat seemed very interested in my skinny little body. Questions again: 'Have you ever had measles, scarlet fever, sore throats?' and [a] lot of other names I had never heard of. I said 'no' to all questions. Requesting that I lay on a leather couch, he put a long thing in his ears, and with a long rubber tube with a thing on the end, tested my chest, back, and belly, tapping with his fingers. 'Take deep breaths' [he ordered, then started] examining my eyes, nose, ears, throat, and [then he was] telling me to 'stand up and bend over'. [I heard him] saying: 'I want to look up your rear.' It was very embarrassing having somebody you don't know looking at, and sticking his finger up, my bum. Then he took hold of my balls, mumbling something. I took off like a rabbit across the room. Blime, my balls were very sore after. The Doctor said, 'What did you do that for?' I replied, 'What did you say?' The Doctor said, 'Cough'. [I said] 'Blime, I understood you to say "Off".' I was lucky not to have lost them.

Patting me on the shoulder, he said, 'You have passed the exam. Although you are very thin and narrow chested, you are wiry and in fairly good health. [You need] regular food, plenty of drill, warm uniforms, [and then] you will make the grade. Off you go. Next man.'

I was sent to an Army man with three other blokes. He lined us up and told us we would have to take the oath of allegiance, and 'swear by the almighty God [that] you will fight for his Majesty the King, his heirs, all his kids and relations'. At least that what I thought he was talking about and with 'swelt [so help] me God', we handed back the bibles. And I was thinking that a pro is [apropos his] book, I wonder if Father Marlarky would approve [of] them holding that bible.

Giving us all a new shilling, [he was] saying, 'You are now in the Army. You have a very wide choice of regiments to choose from.' Facing me, the Soldier said: 'Your education qualifications are very low, and the only choice you have is the PBI.' 'Is that a regiment?', said me. 'No, me Lad, it means the Poor Bloody Infantry. Have you a choice?' 'Well', I answered, […] seeing I was a RC, and had an Irish Name, [the Soldier advised], 'You are a Cockney Irish. I would suggest you choose the Royal Dublin Fusiliers.' [I said] 'You have talk[ed] me into it mate, so the Royal Dubs it is. Now I am ready. When do I sail for France?'

[The Soldier began] explaining [that] I had to undergo training in drill, with rifles, firing them, running around the Barrack square, route marching: 'It all takes about three months to make you a front-line Soldier, experienced in the arts of War. I am sending you to the City of Cork in the South of Ireland. Here is a warrant for the train to Fishguard and [you will go] across the Irish sea on the ferry boat. Here is your food warrants. Go home, say goodbye to Mum and Dad, report to RTO Euston Station at 6.30 two nights from now.'

On his way home, he wondered what his Mum would say. Had he done the right thing in going to War? Would his Mum tell the Army he was under-age? With these thoughts going through his mind, and facing the very cold [weather] and rain, with the shilling in his pocket, he arrived home. His Mum was getting the tea ready. His old man was drinking his ale at the corner pub just around the corner. It was called the Lilyput Arms. Mum was frying about six or seven bloaters, that is, smoked herring in the old black frying [pan], and when he told her what he had done, [she began] leaving the fire and wiping her hands on the sack apron. My Mother [… said] 'You will not be going into the Army. You are too young, and this war will mean there will be plenty of work about, so tomorrow you will go and give them back their shilling. Wait till your Father gets home. He will not be pleased.' But Mum was wrong. My Dad was very mellow, and when I told him what I had done, and that I had joined the Dublin Fus., he nodded his head and said, 'That is a bloody good regiment.' My Dad and Mum were both from the County of Limerick, and just a few miles from Cork, and when I showed him the new Shilling, he said to Mum, 'Give him the can and we will drink to the bloody Dublins.' I went to the Pub and, for tuppence, the tin can was filled with a black beer porter (mum's favourite drink). The can held a quart, and [...] all [my] brothers and sisters drank and they all wished me good luck.

Next day he told his Mum that the Soldier told him he could leave his Mum an allotment of sixpence a day, and the Army would pay her 15 shillings every week while he was in the Army. That made her very happy. 15 shillings was a very lot of money in those days. It would mean more food and clothes would be available for my Brothers and Sisters. (There were only four of us at home.[7] Two brothers were in Australia.)

[*He goes to the railway station.* Circa 400 words]

[Later, I found myself] boarding the Fishguard express and finding a third class compartment with about seven other blokes. They (like him) were on their way to join the Dubs. We were a very merry crowd. Most were Irish, who (as they said) hated the English govt. and they did not like the Germans. As one of them told me, he loved a fight. I was the butt of some good-humoured banter, some saying it was a sacrilege [that] a low-down bloody London Cockney should be allowed to join a famous Irish regiment that fought in the Boer War, India and other god-forgotten places, with battle honours on their flags. This good natured [banter] was to stay with him right through this military service. They shared smokes, food, and even money, and at stops made merry in the bars.

[*He arrives at Victoria Barracks, Cork.* Circa 600 words]

Later, the rest of the Platoon came in from their training, for dinner. They had been square-bashing since early morn with a break for

breakfast. They showed us newcomers how to arrange our kits in the
regulation manner and told us we could expect a kit inspection by our
Platoon Officer. [They] gathered around asking questions: where we
came from? They were all Irishmen straight from the bogs — at least
that's what they were telling us. I was the one that came in for their
attention. I started to talk, and as soon as I opened my mouth, one big
[soldier] with one stripe on his arm [...] started: 'Oh Mother of God!
Is this Regiment so hard-up, they have to recruit the dregs of London?
Look at him! He's too bloody thin to cast a shadow, and if he stood side-
ways you couldn't see him.' This made [me] quite mad, and [I started]
yelling at the Lance Corporal: 'Are you looking for a fight? If so, come
outside, and I'll give [you] a bleeding hiding. You may be big, [but] my
motto is "the bigger they are, the harder they fall". I am not scared of
any of you blokes, you big Irish slobs!' A roar of laughter greeted his
outburst. Three or four moved in on him and, gathering a blanket from
the bed, spread it on the floor, then tossed me almost to the rafters. I
was helpless when they finished. Then giving him some hard slaps on
his bum, ruffled his hair which was fairly lengthy (not being able to
afford the penny [that] the Barber charged for cutting), [they said] 'You
are accepted and welcome to our Platoon.'

[*He describes training in Cork*. Circa 850 words]

The three months training passed very quickly. I became very
friendly with all my Mates, and was given some training with the bicy-
cling section. They issued me with a bloody great big heavy bicycle, and
after parades we went riding for a few miles. All in the course of training, we were allowed to take our machines out for our own pleasure.
Our Cycle Sgt. [told us] to get as much riding as possible: 'It will come
in handy when you are in France.' By this means, I was able to see a
great deal of the countryside around about Cork. What amazed [me]
was the very friendliness of the local people — being thirsty, you rode
to a little farm-house and asked for a drink of water, and they always
gave me buttermilk, and sometimes a cup of tea. The people were very
poor. [They wore] old clothes and sometimes the women and girls wore

no boots. I thought they were worse [off] than my Mum and Dad in London. We could go and look at shops, watch the horse traffic, [and listen to] the big farm carts that always drove in the middle of the night, but those friendly people had nowhere to go at night. [They could] only [go] to bed. They were interested in my [talking] to them about London. They reckoned [that] although I spoke in a strange voice, they liked to [hear] my tales about London. […]

One Sunday, [I was] visiting a family that offered me a cup of tea with homemade bread and butter. I did not like the butter (it was very salty and not as good as the margarine Mum used to buy for a penny for 4 ozs) and while talking and eating there were about 9 [people] including the Mother and Father (all the Kids were steps and stairs in ages). [Suddenly], without warning, a Priest walked in. He was not as well dressed [as] Father Marlarky. He wore very shabby clothes and his dog collar was not too clean. He started off with 'God Bless all.' This Priest was about as big as me but much fatter. The husband of the house was big, broad, and well over six ft. tall. His Priest said in a very angry voice, 'You were not at Mass today, and did not receive the Holy Communion. Why?' The man said, 'Excuse me, Father' and went outside. He was followed by the Holy Man. I heard angry words and then the [priest] reached up, slapped the man's face [and] said, 'Bend over', and kick[ed] the poor bloke right up his arse and this fellow just stood and took it, from the little Holy Man. I then saw the wife hand two pennies to him.

[*Casey is charged for addressing an officer as 'mate' and punished by seven days' 'defaulters', that is, 'peeling spuds, scrubbing the cook house … cleaning out the poop houses, and wash rooms'.* Circa 340 words]

I have just one more incident to record before leaving the City of Cork as a wiry, very fit, and very well trained Royal Dublin Fusilier. On one of my nights meandering through the well-lit streets, and still enjoying the crowds of people that were shopping etc., I noticed a very nice-looking girl. She had a beautiful crop of very dark raven hair, with a nice oval smiling face. I spoke to her and, as she seemed willing to talk, I was telling her I would be soon sailing to France, and she was the first Irish Girl who I had asked to go for [a] walk with me. We spent a couple of hours just walking and talking. We arranged to meet again and for the next few weeks we discussed everything: Did I go to Mass? Would she be able to see me when the Regiment marched on Church parade? Oh, the Church parade was a wonderful sight: up to 600 men in four Companies, four abreast, heads held high, eyes darting right and left to the smile and waves of the people. I did notice my dark-eyed, and dark Irish Colleen. She went to the same mass and we use to meet in the Sunday afternoons. One night she failed to keep an appointment with me. Later I was told by her young Brother [that] she had be[en] set on by a gang of the local boys, and they had cut off her lovely hair, because she was associating with a British Soldier. I was most upset and my mates felt very sorry for [me], and said if they knew who did the terrible job, they would get what was coming to them.

[*He describes training.* Circa 160 words]

Just before leaving for the front, I was taken by the friends I had made to kiss the blarney stone. It was a great Irish custom. The stone was down a kind of a wall. Two strong men held you by the ankles and with your head bumping [against] the side you kissed this well-smoothed lump of stone. To all and sundry, he who kisses the Blarney stone will have wit, gift of the gab, and live to a ripe old age. It was just an old woman's tale.

Yarning at night when we were all broke waiting for payday, the platoon started to talk of their love conquests, and one of my mates said to me, 'Casey, have you ever dipped your wick?' [I asked] 'What do you mean? I ain't got no wick to dip.' When the laughter had subsided, they put it more bluntly: 'Had I ever made love to a girl?' When I said 'no', [they said] 'Oh you must be a bloody virgin, and when we get to France we will soon remedy that!' And one of the blokes said, 'If the French tarts are as tall as our Irish Girls, Casey will have to lug a brick to stand on, if he wants to have a blow through. He will be too short to kiss her tits.' This made me very angry, and I shouted: 'I ain't going to have no

truck with no French tarts. The Priest for the Battalion when I went to
confession told me these Girls were very dirty and they would give
[me] the pox if I went with them. It is a mortal sin to do bad things to
Girls. I had to wait till I was married. And, when I was young, Father
Marlarky told us kids we were never to play Mothers and fathers, but
some of [us] did in the dark porches on our houses.'

These big Irishmen were impressed [with my words] and at the way
I explained this problem. The ribaldry stopped when he told these
Mates of his [that] he was meeting this Irish girl after church Parade on
Sunday, and she would take him to home to have tea with her Mum and
Dad.

The training went on day after day, and although I say [it] to myself,
this bloody little Cockney was as good as the rest of the squad in picking [up] the rudiments of the drill and the musketry exercises. The
training at last began to show just how I was progressing. Regular good
food, and sleep. In fact he was so tired at the end of the day, he was too
tired to play with himself in bed.

[*General descriptions of military training and his progress in courting his girlfriend.* Circa 400 words]

I was still seeing my Irish Girl, and her short hair seem[ed] to me an
improvement on the long hair she lost when the young Sinn Feiners[8] cut
the hair off. Sunday in Ireland was very much the same as in Canning
Town: all the Irishmen after attending the 12 o'clock Mass, made a bee-
line for the pubs. When I met my Girl at the rendezvous, she was my
little Irish Colleen (the name his mates called their Girls). I say 'little',
[but] she was at least three inches taller and weighed at least 2 stone
[more than me]. Her short hair was raven black with a tinge of gold.
She reminded me of my sister Biddy who was also a dark-haired beauty.
Me old Man when he was in his cups often remarked that I was the runt
of the 16 kids he had sired and I was the only one like me Mother who
was very small and dainty.

[My colleen was always] greeting me with the words: 'My, you do
look very smart and handsome. If only you were a little taller and had

more flesh on your small bones, I could refer [to] you then as my Tall Handsome Soldier. Even though you are suppose to be an enemy of Ireland (that [is] why those louts cut my hair), I am not sorry nor am I ashamed. I like you, and you are the first boy I have ever walked out with.'

I was very pleased at those thoughts. We spent a pleasant time in the saloon bar at the pub. I was in funds as my mates chipped in with a few coppers each. My Beauty had a port and lemon (port wine with lemonade). I had a pint of porter. We stayed drinking till closing [time], and [then went] walking around the very lovely harbour with dozens of young couples arm in arm till tea time. It was a very lovely day for me and [...] I asked her, 'did she have a bike?' She had, and for the whole time I was in training (every Sunday after Mass) we went cycling through the countryside. Till the time of my departure for the Front, Agnes never missed our Sunday outing. The funny part of our rides [was when] I was told always to take the lead. When I asked why, [she] replied, 'It is sinful to ride in front of a Boy, [who might be] looking at my ankles and my back. [It] rouses sinful thoughts in your mind, and makes you think of bad things.'

[*He describes training.* Circa 440 words]

It was at this stage of my military service [that] I received my first letter addressed: Pte. E. Casey, no 17787, B Company, Royal Dublin Fus. Victoria Barracks, Cork. It was from my dark Colleen and it made me very sad. It told him: 'Again I was attacked by Men and Girls.' She [was] almost stripped again, [they] called her 'a British Soldier's Moll' and 'whore', and [since] she did not heed the first lesson and [was] a disgrace to her family and Ireland, if she did not leave Cork, more trouble was inevitable. [The letter continued] 'So this is farewell. I am going to Liverpool where my Sister will look after me. There is plenty of work, and I will write you soon. I feel very worried, Ned, at your near departure for France. God protect [you] in the battles to come. It is not your fault [that] I am in this position. I did not think that bigotry was so prevalent in my native land. It is very fashionable to hate the English, especially the Soldiers — saying they were invaders. [They make] no comment on the very large numbers of Irishmen who took the King's shilling and proved they were ready and willing to give their lives for their Country.'

History has proved the little Irish Girl was right in her thinking. When I read the letter to my Mates, I told them I would survive the war. I had the gift of the gab. I had kissed the blarney stone and I was not afraid.

[*He describes life in camp.* Circa 710 words]

I was still able to visit my various friends in the earth-floor cottages, and enjoy the buttermilk and the lovely home-made bread. The home-made butter was very salty and to be polite I had to say it was lovely. There were hordes of kids of all ages and sizes running almost naked, but it was fun to give them rides on my bike. It was with great pride that I was introduced to the 'Gentleman who paid the rent and provided the food'. It was a bloody great pig! To me, it was the size of a pony. It was a friendly pig and allowed me to tickle his ears. I got to love these Irish people. I was thrilled with their broad Irish Brogue and their great joke was to say, 'Arru from Cork?' I had to reply with my cockney accent, 'Yerra gods know I am. Aru?'

I got a letter from my old Mother (it was the first I had got) telling me the allotment was payable every week and Dad was now working overtime and we now have plenty of food and Dad was now able to have a drop of rum now and again. I was also told in the letter I had an Aunt (her Sister) living at a town called Kilmallock in the County of Limerick. I went and told my Company Officer about the letter, and he arranged for me to have a weekend pass to visit them. A weekend pass for troops was a rare privilege for Troops under intensive training before embarking for the Front. On receipt of a leave pass [and] a rail warrant, I packed an haversack. All my mates had a whip round to help pay expenses — about 2 bob. [They were all] wishing me 'God's speed'. [I was] thinking [that] things were a little [better] when they knew I had relatives [in] Limerick. I was now one of them and no longer an invader.

It was (if my memory serves [me] right) about 40 miles from Cork and I rode the Dublin Express. [...] Although some of the passengers gave me stony stares [and] conversation was not encouraged, [...] at Mallow Junction (which was in the County of Munster) a band of women presiding over a stall on the platform were giving the troops from the train, tea, cakes, etc, and it made me think there were some folks in Southern Ireland [who] were doing their bit for the troops.

[I found myself] arriving at the town of Kilmallock, and walking through the narrow streets with their small stone houses [which were] all close together (just like Canning Town). The Locals did not look very friendly and [when] asking where my Aunt lived [...] two or three people ignored me and continued to walk on. I felt worried. Seeing a priest in [a] very shabby black coat and skirt (it was the first [time] I had seen a priest dressed like him) he gave me the information and walked me to the house where my Aunt lived. In conversation, he told me [that] this town was a Sinn Fein stronghold, and he supported his flock, and that my Cousin was an Officer in the Limerick company. [He said] 'I will take you in. I will be interested in his reactions [to the fact that] he has a very close blood relation who is on the other side. The Irishmen who have joined their Arch-enemy to fight Germans in our opinion are Mercenaries and traitors.'

He took me in[to] the house without knocking, and when my Aunt (who is a widow) saw us together, [she] said in her deep Irish Limerick brogue: 'And what in the name of God are [you] bringing into my house? A British Soldier! And I'm telling you Father, he is not welcome.' Then my Cousin came from out [of] the back room. He was a big fellow and about my age. When the introductions were over, he asked his Mother to make a cup of tea. The atmosphere in the room was very chilly. Four of us sat around the room, latter joined by another cousin, a buxom beautiful girl, [a] little older than her Brother. The Priest dominated the conversation. It was very anxious time for me. They were the only Relations I have known. But they accepted me, as a relation. But in my own mind I had the feeling that I was only tolerated because I was (in a way) family.

As conversation developed it was my feminine Cousin who was the most radical. Her love for Ireland and her rabid hatred of England [was strong. I heard her] remarking that if those protestant majority in Ulster would only co-operate with the Catholics in the South 'we would be a united Country and compel the English to give us freedom by granting home rule for a united Ireland'. Of course, her views were accepted by the majority, and it made me feel I was regarded as an antagonist, but, by the time the tea party was over, [...] the suggestion came from the Priest, [who said] 'Why not take your Cousin down to the local, and let the rest of your Company look him over?'

Walking down this small town [with] narrow streets, me in uniform [and with] Shamas who towered over me, was an experience that still remains [in my mind]. The locals (Men, Women, and barefoot kids) looked on with anger and I thought trouble was looming, but I was wrong. Shamas remarked, 'Sure, take no heed. When they know you are my Mother's Nephew, you will be accepted. I feel very sorry for you. The Germans are going to win this War, and we (us Sinn Feiners, both Men and Women) will do all we can to help.' And he recited for my benefit the doggerel that was very popular in the southern part of [this] lovely part of the Erin Isle.

> 'Ireland will be Ireland,
> When England was a Pup.
> and Ireland will be Ireland.
> When England is buggered up.'

The climax of our fairly long walk ended when we both entered the small bar, which was crowded. Shamus ordered two pints of Porter, and since I was flush with money (I had over half [a] crown) I offered to pay. 'No', said my Cousin, 'ye are my guest, ye are my Kin, you are welcome to our food and bed.' He then made a little speech telling his friends who I was, and finished with the words, 'Blood is thicker than water, and like someone said on the Cross, "we forgive you, ye know not what ye do".'

I had a wonderful week-end. Cousin Margaret took me cycling, borrowing Shamas' bike. Like my little Girlfriend in Cork, I had to take the lead. After 12 o'clock mass on the Sunday and the usual session at the local, [I was] feeling very nicely, thank you. We got home and had the usual roast rabbit and trimmings. Walking me to the station, this Sinn Feiner Captain told me [that] serious trouble was ahead for the English. [He told me that] Kilmallock used to be a Garrison Town. On the outbreak of war, the English Regiment stationed [there] was sent to France, so the Barrack remained empty 'till me and my Company will take it over'. [He said] 'The local RIC [Royal Irish Constabulary] turned a blind eye to our activities knowing their days were numbered.' I was a worried little Man when I arrived back, and told my Mates all that had happened. It was generally accepted that the troubles [would] break out before the end of the war.

Thinking back to my memorable weekend with the Irish branch of the Family: in conversation with Shamas, he seemed very interested in London saying 'how in the name of God and his blessed Mother' did his Uncle Dinny (my Dad) allow me, ('and look at you, you are almost a midget, thin, with not an ounce of meat on your bones!') join the British Army? [He said] 'London must be very hard up [...] for cannon fodder to accept you as a fighting Man. We in this small town [are] small in numbers, but very big in patriotic fervour.'

This statement made me very angry, and [I] then said, 'Did you know, Shamas, at least 95 [per cent] of my regiment, The Royal Dubs., are Southern Irishmen, and a bunch of finest men that ever drank a pint of porter, and I'm proud to be call their Mate.'

Shamas replied: 'There are traitors and renegades in every country. You have them in Britain. Lots of Men and women would rather love than fight. It is poverty [that makes them enlist], inspired by your bloody Government at Westminster who for years and [years] trodden the poor Irish people in the mud. No work, no money. And England [is] full of Irish people who were forced to emigrate. The same applies to America. It is better to leave your homeland, than starve. You, Edward, are not really an English Man. You are [a] full-blooded Irish man, born in the wrong place.'

[I replied] 'Now look Shamas, I ain't no Irishman. I am a full-blooded Cockney, born in Canning Town a mile or so from the Bow bells, and in the biggest City in the whole bleeding world, and I mean the World. I cannot understand why you have such hatred for us English so much. You may have your reasons, as I have mine.'

People were looking at [us], and going into the local pub. I said to my cousin, 'Come on, lets have a drink.' [My cousin said] 'Well, well, you little Leprechaun, I'll have a pint. Mine's an 'alf, and I'm paying.' [I said] 'What, again! you spalpeen [rascal]? You paid last time. And what's a Leprechaun, it must be a wicked word.' 'Oh no', replied himself, 'he's one of the little people of Ireland and they live in the forests and sleep under toad stalls.' 'Garn, you are kidding', [I exclaimed]. 'Yes, I am', [he said].

When one man, asked Himself who the hell was I, Shamas repeated, 'This is my First Cousin from London. He is my Mother's Sister's Boy. And I'll have you treat him with respect. If you don't, I'll ask you all to come outside and take your coats off and fight.' I stood up to my full 5 feet something, and shouted, 'By God, I'll give you a hand to fight the buggers, and I say "the bigger you are the harder you will fall!"' This remark was greeted with laughter and by the time they finished patting [me] on the back, [I] was stiff and sore. Even Shamas seemed very happy at this turn of events: it put him 'on side' with his mates who by now understood the position. As far as I was concerned, I was some poor fella, and because I was poor and had very little money, [and was] out of work, [and] a bit of a burden on my family, I took the King's Shilling and my Mother got an allotment of 15-shillings a week.

A murmur of approval greeted my statement. 'How come,' said the second in command of his company, 'your Cousin is named Casey?' [My cousin replied] 'A very good question, Mr O'Rorke. It was just a case of one Casey marrying another Casey. I don't remember that marriage. We are not sure when and where the marrying took place. It seems his Mother wanted her Son to meet this branch of the Family. His Father we understand was working in Dublin, and my mother's Sister must have been working there.'

On the way home [I was] feeling very mellow, with the porter inside [me]. They sat down to dinner [and I was] saying to [my] Aunt, 'Don't you ever have other meats besides rabbit? It is very tasty, with all the trimmings, and I am curious.' [She replied] 'Shamas, we cannot afford to buy meat, it is too dear, so we have a bit of a raid on the queer fellow's land up the hill. He is a very wealthy Englishman and lives well on the rents he charges for all these houses, and on Fridays we go out at night and tickle his trout. Sure, Edward, they are lovely to eat.' I said, 'I've [never] tasted trout. We only have herring, kippers and some[times] a haddock.'

[He returns to London for a few days' leave. Circa 135 words]

I got a wonderful welcome from my Mum and Dad. I (with some others) were the heroes of Kerry Street, and the day before our leave ended the street put on a real Cockney Party. There was beer, food, singing and dancing. Those who had pianos carried them out into the street and, along with fiddles and of course mouth organs, [we had a good time] — one bloke even played the jews harp. And in some cases a little love was going on in the darkened porches. Sitting around the fire in the kitchen [was] my Dad ([he] was on the Night Shift, starting at 10 pm.), [and he] promised to give me a call as I was to leave early. Mum asked how did I get on with her people in Limerick, and [I] told her that her Sister was a very attractive Woman, but not so beautiful as his old Mum.

His money lasted longer than he expected and his Mum said the 15 shillings was a god-send. It enabled her to buy more food and clothes for his brothers and Sisters. His Dad was getting more wages on account of the War, by working overtime. The younger members had all gone to bed. He said, 'Mum, how come I was born so small, and all my life as far as I can remember I have [been] skinny, not robust like some of the others.' It hurts to be the runt of the family. My two Brothers in Australia were fairly big men.

Mum said, […] 'When you were born, Ned, […] you almost died. You were very tiny, but you gave me a hard time. The midwife saved your life. She grabbed hold of you when you stopped breathing, held you like a plucked chicken by the legs, put the cold water tap on full bore over the sink. Then suddenly comes the biggest cry from a baby that I have ever heard. The Midwife said, "He will be right now and there is nothing wrong with his lungs." It was drastic but it worked.'

[In] those early days in the east end of London (according to my Mum), Doctors rarely attended childbirth. Women had to rely on Mid-wives who were very good but untrained. The hospital was the work-house infirmary at Whips-Cross, about 5 miles away.

I replied, 'Gor blimy, what a time you must have had. Now I know why I am such a dumb cluck. I will never be big and strong. I think I have filled out a bit since I joined up, don't you?'

[*He returns to Cork, via Holyhead*. Circa 165 words]

He spent a very pleasant day strolling the narrow streets of this lit-tle Welsh town of Holyhead. His uniform was an open invitation to the pubs, and some of the locals invited him to their homes. He reluctantly refused. He was happy just strolling. Going into a tea room, his dinner was 'on the house'. The Lady running the shop told him she knew he had little money, and it [was] a great pleasure to serve one who was soon to leave for the front. He loved the Welsh accent: it was so dif-ferent from the Irish brogue.

He met with a fair girl who offered to show him the sights of the town and, walking him to the top of the hill overlooking the very attrac-tive little harbour, [they] spent some hours lying on the grass. She told him it would [be] late and dark before the train from London arrived. She was a bold girl, who made all the advances. It was my very first sex-ual experience, and although […] getting it seem[ed] to take a hell of a time, the twilight in North Wales is very lovely, and lying on the grass with such a lovely Girl, who (by the way she was acting) was feeling very clucky. She was a lovely kisser, and that's all she wanted to do, and when my hand started to roam she stiffened up and murmured, 'No, I just enjoy lying with you. It makes me feel very nice, but anything else […] must wait till I find Mr. Right.' She gave me her name and I promised to write from France, but I lost the slip of paper.

On the way back to Town, she held my arm [and said], 'I am very proud to be seen with such a good looking Soldier. Life is very dull in this little town, and enjoyment is at a premium. I am just turned 22, and [...] never been kissed til tonight, and you are a very good kisser, Edward.'

He blushed and told her she was the first Girl he had taken out since his unfortunate experience in Cork some weeks earlier. 'Oh my dear, have I rarlly found a virgin?' [she exclaimed]. [He said] 'A Virgin? What's a virgin? The only Virgin I know of is the Blessed Virgin Mary. Since I have been in the Army, I have heard so many new words which frankly I don't understand.'

The Girl then said, 'Let's change the subject, and tell me about yourself. What's it like being in the Army? Sure it must be very thrilling — marching, firing rifles, promenading through the City of Cork, on Saturday night going to dances, and cuddling the Girls when you take them home.'

He told her, 'Irish Girls are not like that. They are very religious. They go to Mass and confession, and they won't let you kiss or cuddle them. They fight you off and say "When we are married, we will do all the bad things then." It is sinful to harbour bad thoughts, and I am very sorry I felt like [I] did when we were on the grass.'

They were walking slowly towards the Ferry Wharf, [the Girl] remarking: 'We two are like ships passing in the night. We may never meet again, and I will always cherish this meeting. Some day, somewhere, after this war is over, and you survive, you will meet up with some very pretty Girl, get married and have family. What comes natural to some Boys, makes you afraid and you then go to your priest and confess your most intimate thoughts. Just fancy going through life with no fun.'

She kissed him a fond goodbye.

[*After a brief stay in Ireland, he is sent to Le Havre.* Circa 855 words]

I had a wonderful time on my first day in a foreign country. My five francs did not buy very much reason. A Frenchman who spoke English pointed to some of the highlights, like Churches [and] shops, and he told me I should visit a cafe called the White Star. I found it and although it was late afternoon, it was brightly lighted with rows of electric light bulbs. When I got inside, the place was crowded with Troops (mostly French) and just a few Tommys. Sitting at an empty table [was] a lovely young pretty girl, and all this Girly wore was a kind of cheese-cloth wrap-around, pinned at the shoulder. That girl (to my embarrassment) exposed every private part of her body. With my breath coming in little short pants, I said I would like a drink. Her broken English was lovely to listen to and sounded so funny. She bought me a bottle of wine, and it tasted [like] vinegar. It was so sour. I was told later by some locals it was termed a dry wine and was the national drink for the French Troops, which they called poilurs[9], or something like that. And bang went 75 centimes, and that was all I had left from my pay. This very bold Girl then sat on my knee with her arm around my [shoulders] and exposing one of her titties. [She] told me she would give me a lovely time and take me to one of the small cubicles that was all around the walls of the Whore House (that's [what] my mates told me it was) and when I told her [that] the wine took all my money, not believing me, she searched all my pockets. I was in a dreadful state, for when she stood up to search me I could see the fair hair around her business. Satisfied I was telling the truth, she called over the bloke on the door who was dressed like an Admiral with all the gold lace on his long coat and around his cap. He made very short work of giving the Bums' rush [throwing me out], and told me never to come to this place unless I had money to pay for my fun. So back to camp in my usual condition 'broke to the wind' [penniless]. I did not mention my experience to my Mates. You know its awful to be broke, and when people say 'Money is the root of all evil', I did sincerely wish that some of those roots would enter my pockets.

[*He makes money by stealing and then selling boxes of cigarettes.* Circa 105 words]

With such a large sum in my pockets, and thoughts of that well-lighted palace of joy, and the urgent feeling in my [*illegible*] I found myself being propelled towards the White Star. The Admiral was still the doorkeeper. I knew as he walked towards me [that] he recognised me [as] the Tommy he gave the bums' rush to. I had to show him my money before he would let me come [in]. The Brothel was still crowded and by the look of Couples coming and going into the little room, business was brisk. Before I could find an empty table and sit, a different [Girl] took charge of me, leading me along, talking in her funny English, and wearing the same dress. Seating us at a table near the action-rooms, [she said] 'Would my little and very handsome and little Tommy, like to buy me a drink?' I said, 'No, but I will have a beer.' The beer was weak: it would never make you randy no matter how much you drank. In fact, we called it 'love in a boat'. This lovely looking Girl followed the same routine as her mate did: sitting on my knee, kissing my cheek (never my lips), and rubbing the nipples of her tits on my face, across my lips, all in view of the crowds of men who were doing the same thing. [She began] putting her hands inside my fly, and murmuring, 'Oh Darling, you are so hard and big. You will like a short time with me. I am very good, and I make you very pleasurable. Drink your beer, and come.'

We had to wait a while for an empty room. When we got in, [we were] stand[ing] very close, [and she was] taking down my pants. I was amazed when she took hold of my business and examined it very carefully. Satisfied [that] I was clean and free from the Gonna [*gonorrhoea*], [she] laid on the bed. Her bit of cheese[-cloth] was off, [and she was] opening wide her lovely white legs. She was more plump than the first one. Her large breasts sagged a little. I was told to lay on top of her. Then my trouble started. I went limp, and though this French hussy tried everything she knew (even putting my thing in her mouth), I could not get hard. Then she got very angry: 'Am I not very beautiful to you, that you do not want to love me? You English are very cold and do not know how to make love. I leave you now. Get dressed, I have work to do.'

When I asked her for my five francs [back that] I [had] paid her (because I had not had any pleasure), well! the way she acted, and [she was] screaming French abuse [...] although I could not understand a word she screamed. And forgetting her cheese-dress, [she] stormed out and, as she went out, the Admiral rushed in [yelling]: 'What's the trouble? Oh! its you again. Didn't you have enough money again?' I said, 'I paid my five francs for a blow thru, and was not able to get hard, so I demand my money back.' The look on the Admiral's face, and the angry way he got his arms about [the] scrub of my neck, the other hand on the seat of my pants [got me] thinking '[it's] the Bum's rush again'. I was soon on the street again, [listening to] the Admiral telling the watching crowd what had happened, and the words [he said were]: 'He wanted his money back because he could not get hard!' [The Admiral was] glaring into my face, saying, 'It takes a real man to love a Woman. Go away and grow up.' Thus ended my first experience in Love. I did not tell my mates of my failure. I was still a joke in the platoon, and to confess what happened would have made it worse.

[*He spends time in the trenches, followed by a rest period behind the lines.* Circa 1,140 words]

After the rest period, it was back to the trenches doing the same old chores. Our Company Commander (I was told) was going on leave and [wanted] a souvenir to take home and it had to be a length of German barbed wire, and our platoon was detailed to go out into No Man's Land [to] cut him the bit of wire. The Platoon Officer lined us up and said, 'I want about 4 volunteers to do this little job.' Nobody moved or walked to the front. After a while and walking along as if he was inspecting us, he pointed and said, 'You, you, and you, will come along with me tonight. You will cut an opening in the line of our barbed wire and come back to the trench. Each man will be given wire cutters.' I was one of the very unlucky blokes to be picked, and I was really scared. I could not show it, and I had to act as if it was an everyday job to go into no man's land and cut a bit of wire so that our Major could show it to his old woman, [and] she would be so proud of his bravery [that] she would let him have a bit of grummet (that's what some Irishmen called the 'blow-thru'). I hoped he would be like me, and when she was on her back waiting for him to up her, he could not get a hard on.

Anyway, we knew what we had to do: 'so for Christ's [sake] let's get it over.' There were six in the party: [a] Lieut., Sgt., and 4 Tommys. The night was as dark as the inside of a cow, which suited us. It was easy to cut a passage through our wire, but the German's wire was very hard and the spikes seemed longer. I made a half-hearted attempt to cut the wire [but] it was too tough or my hand was too weak. I could hear the Germans talking. Getting the wind up, I crawled to the opening in the wire and waited. All of a sudden 3 or 4 Very Lights[10] [lit up] the sky [and] we all froze till they went. Then the machine-guns started. I knew by experience [that] if you buried your head in the mud [and] remained very still, the bullets ([which were] about waist-high) flew over your head. The blitz did not last long. I heard the slithering bodies coming towards me, [and I found myself] joining them. Not one of them thought I [was] helping them. Anyhow, we did get back to our own lines, and the Major was waiting, and the Officer was the only [one] that had a sample, which made me think I was not the only one to renege on the exercise.

So time went on till one day the Germans sent over a shell barrage which lasted for hours. The whole front was lit up from the flashes from guns — [everything] from the small field guns to the big howitzers.[11] They were throwing everything they had at us. Crouching on the fire step, we were ordered into the dugout. I was all of a tremble with fear, or cowardice, call it what you will. I lay on the damp floor, covered myself with sandbags, [and] holding my rosary beads and reciting the Hail Marys, [heard myself] saying to myself, 'Casey, you are doomed. I will never come out of this hole alive.'

I felt the ceiling falling on me and when I woke up, it was in a hospital. I felt so clean, feeling the sheets around, and [yet] still the sound of guns firing [could be heard]. Off I went again. I was told that I jumped out of the bed and tried to get out of the window, but I felt strong hands around my shoulders [and] I felt a prick in my arm, and [fell into a deep] sleep again. I was told by the Doctor that for some weeks I lay in a state of shock. I had lost my memory, did not know who

I was [or] what Regiment I belonged [to] but not to worry: 'It will take a little time, just rest and relax.'

[I asked] 'Doctor, I was in the trenches: am I wounded?'

He replied, 'No, you have been badly shell shocked, and [are] suffering from acute neurarasine [*neurasthenia*]. This neurotic condition may last some time, but take the medicine we give you, and [we will] find [out] who you are, [and] where you come from. You will be able tell us in your own good time.'

The days went by: I was eating well but sleeping badly. Conversing with Nurses and other Patients, they told me I was a very sick Tommy. I had nightmares, and one night I walked out of the ward door, went to the yard (it was freezing night), [and] I climbed up the gutter pipe. [I] was seen from a ward window, on the roof. They rescued me, gave me a drink of rum, [and] wrapped me in hot water bottles. From then on, I was always under supervision. I heard some talk [that] I was to be transferred to Conly [*Colney*] Hatch, a mental Hospital in London. I was given physio treatment, and I gradually recovered. I was very worried at the thought of being confined to a mad House. I kept repeating to myself, '[I] am not crazy. I will get better.'

At time[s] his mind went back his sojourn in the trenches, wondering about his mates: were they still alive? In the wards, he listened to the conversation of the wounded Patients and some were very badly hit. Some had lost arms, legs etc, and the strange part of this war was the utmost cheerfulness of those who had lost limbs. All of them were considering how they would cope in Civvy Street, and would they be able to find work, and all would conclude, 'Thank Christ, I will be out of the Army, and could not be sent overseas again.'

[*His health slowly improves and he is given seven days' leave.* Circa 1,800 words]

I was home the next day. Mum, Dad and Brothers and sisters gave me a wonderful welcome. That night we experienced an air raid, and it was mostly in the East End the bombs were dropped. I got a bad relapse, during the noise of anti-aircraft guns that were around the docks (Victoria [Dock] and Albert [Dock]). I crawled under the bed, trembling and crying. I had the proper wind up. The comfort I received from Mum helped me a lot.

Most of his leave he spent in the West End [of London]. The train from Tidal Basin to Liverpool St. [took] only 20 minutes and from there to Picadilly Circus was my favourite spot. Then [he liked] Charing Cross Road, Trafalgar Sq, [and] Hyde Park corner with its scruffy orators telling the world their views of all its troubles. [He was] feeling as if he was one of the boys. Everybody was friendly, and strangely it was the men in civvies who wanted (and did) buy him beer, food, and invitations to their flats. Sometimes it was a ten bob note that was slipped into his hand with the words, 'have one on me'. [I met] Girls who I was fond of calling the Ladies of Joy and of the night. And during [my] meanderings, I would be approached by one of the Girls, saying, 'Are you looking for a naughty little Girl?' He would say, 'Oh, no Dear. It is a sinful act to do bad things to Girls.' One of them remarked in a very tony voice, 'Are you a queen?', [and she] laughed and walked off. One of his ladies, took a liking to him, saying, 'It was your badge with RDF [Royal Dublin Fusiliers] that made me talk to you, but you are not Irish. Why are you in an Irish Regiment?' I then told her how and why I joined the Dubs. [I said] 'Come, my Dear, and I'll buy you a nice cup of tea.' I took this Irish Girly to Lyons Corner House, which in my opinion was the very hum of the Piccadilly. [It was] lovely [and was] called by most of its habituates 'the Dilly'. It was crowded no matter what time [of] day or [however] late [at] night. It was packed with people looking for pick-ups or friends doing the Town. I loved this Corner House.

Back to my Irish Girl. 'Tell me', I asked, 'What part of the old sod do you hail from?' [She said] 'I am Kerry, born and bred, and I'm here in London not to help the English with their War, but to make money.' I then told her how poor my Parents [were], and I joined the Army so that My Old Mother could draw my allotment of 15/– a week. I also joined [an] Irish Regiment because as kids in Kerry Street [we] use to sing a little ditty that went like this:

'Me Mother and Father were Irish,
and I was Irish too,
we bought a kettle for ninepence,
and that was Irish too —

Chorus:

Cock a doodle.
Cock a doodle.
I'm the cock of the North.'

This Girl laughed till the tears ran down her cheeks, and we sat talking for hours ignoring the glares of the Manager (a very severe Lady dressed in black). I used to meet her almost every [day] of my leave, she offered me money, [saying]: 'Half a crown a week is very little pay. It would please me if you would accept a few pounds to spend on yourself. I have learnt to like you, and although I am What I am, You would be very much [wiser] if you was to accept my money, than from those bad men who give you a few shillings. They have a reason, and I'll tell you why. Those men are what we call Queers. They never go and love a woman. They pick a young, nice-looking Boy just like you, give him money so that the Boy will make love to them. Please, Ned, don't have anything to do with those rotten creatures.'

Leaving the Tea Rooms, she took him to a crowded [pub] with troops and Sailors. They sat till closing time. Several men approached the Girl asking would she like a drink, [but she was always] refusing them, saying, 'I'm fixed for the night. Maybe tomorrow.' She was saying, 'Would you like to sleep with me tonight? It will not cost you any money.' 'Oh no', said I, 'I must go home. I can catch the last bus to Barking, it passes Canning Town.' [She asked] 'Tell me, Ned, have you ever loved a Girl?' 'Oh yes', said I, 'in France, the nurses at the hospital, the Titled Lady that took [me] out for tea, the other Women who took [me] to the Zoo and [for] walks in the afternoon, from the Hospital.' [She said] 'Oh No, my dear, I mean *love*, the love you do when you go to bed with a Girl.' I was ashamed to tell [her that] I was not capable to love. His Lady Friend suddenly realized that this young good-looking [boy] was a Virgin and he had never experienced love with a girl. 'How old are you, Ned?', [she asked]. 'Turned 18 yrs', [I answered]. [I then heard her] saying, 'So old, yet so young looking. When do you go back to duty?' [I said] 'I have about 3 days left, and I will be seeing you again, won't I?' [She promised] 'Oh yes, we will meet again tomorrow, but I have to work at night.'

[On the way home, he was] reminiscing on top of the last bus to Canning town, thinking about the Irish prostitute, who sold her [body] like the French [prostitutes]. He was also thinking of the Girl who wiped the face of God, and His image was left on the cloth: her name was Mary Magdalene [and] she was on the game too.[12]

[He returns to his unit, but is charged with insolence, confined to barracks for ten days, and fined three days' pay. He is then given four days' leave in Dublin before being sent to France. Circa 2,180 words]

[I soon found myself] arriving in the Capital Dublin, with joy in my heart and appreciation for that gallant band of Ladies who still dispensed tea and other goodies to the troops passing through Railway Stations. They were a god send to us, but there were still many who were willing to pay excessive prices for their beer and spirits at Railway Refreshments rooms. He had a wonderful time. All Irish people did not hate the British Soldier. I met some very nice Dubliners — some who invited me to their homes. I was still a regular attender at Holy Mass, and [was] going to Holy Communion, and I met some very [nice] Girls while waiting my turn outside the Confessional. But nobody would walk out with me in uniform. I could have had some very attractive Girls of the night and, not being interested [and] thinking it was a great waste of money to pay a shilling for a blow through (why, some of those sinful hussies were asking half a crown for a short time, and ten shillings for all night!) [I did nothing]. But I did like to converse with them in the bars of the pubs. I spent a lot of time on the wharfs talking to the Dock workers who tolerated me, enjoying my Cockney accent, especially when I told them that many years ago my old Dad worked on their wharfs. I was having such a good time, and even in Holy Ireland I was surprised to meet so many Queens, who took me to tea-rooms and shouted meals for me.

My money was dwindling slowly but surely. I was about 5 days over-due on my leave pass. There were very many Red Caps, or Military Police, on patrol. Before, I could pass them with confidence, but now almost being a Deserter I avoided them. [One day], coming from the picture house, two of them requested my pass [and] after examining it said, 'Soldier, you are now absent without leave.' The Red Caps were from a English Mob, stationed at Victoria Barracks. Walking between the two of them, I was put in the Guard room. Quite a number were under arrest, mostly for drunkenness. When they heard my cockney accent, [I heard them] remarking, 'A bleeding Londoner in an Irish mob.' And [during] the two days waiting for the escort from Cork, the [in]mates changed every now and again. One bloke [...] was over six months AWOL [absent without leave] and he expected at least [a] prison sentence when he had his DCM [District Court Martial]. I remarked to him [that] this was my first experience as a Prisoner. And as time rolled [on] it was not going to be the last.

[So here he was], lying on bare boards, with just one very thin blan-ket, no pillow. His boots and tunic were taken away ([why] they did this, he could not fathom). Having little else to do but lie on the bare floor and thinking, 'I've had this bloody Army', and he decided he would try and work to work his ticket. Then he wondered how the bloody [hell] he was going to do it.

He had to leave this problem to a later [date] because an Escort arrived from Cork (a Lance Corp[oral] and a Private). [They were] walking [me] to the Railway Station, and asking Me not to give any trouble, which I promised. [He] duly arriv[ed] at his barracks [and] put in the guard room. At least he was with his Regimental Mates: he was not alone. Three other men were awaiting a DCM [District Court [Martial] — one for desertion [for] over 5 months [and] two for selling on uniform[s], boots, blankets, and rifles to Sein Feiners. I learnt quite a lot about their Sein Fein activities — how [they had been] active Members, and join[ed] the Enemy so that they could steal war material and help their Organisation. In front of me, they spoke of their exploits. [I was] saying to them what a risk they took speaking so freely in front of me. [I was] saying, 'I'm an enemy to you, how you know?' [They replied], 'Oh Whist, you little skin flint. We kill Informers, whether they be Irish or English.' I was horrified that serving Soldiers that had volunteered to Fight Germans could do such things. They mentioned a bloke called Carson who was in Germany forming an Irish Brigade to fight [the] English. [13] I asked them: did they know how many Irish Divisions were in France and other fronts? It did not matter a Tinker's curse to them how many Irishmen were fighting England's battles. [They said] 'We are agin the English Government.' [They wanted to know] what the hell was he doing serving with the Irish. What crime did he commit, that put him in this Guard room. [I was] saying, 'I had me a little Holiday in Dublin, and have [had] such a very nice time. Those Dubliners were very good to me: they gave me meals, beds, and sometimes money. If those bloody Red Caps did not pinch me I would still be there.'

In the morning, the Sgt. of the Guard, with a lot of noise, unlocked the cell door [and yelled] 'Casey! Make yourself presentable. You are for the high jump at 9 am.' Later, when called, he said to the Escort (the usual 2 men and the NCO), 'Take the Prisoner to the Company Orderly Room.' [And so I was marched] between the Escort, the Command, the NCO marching alongside, with the usual left, right, left, right. I thought to myself, 'This bleeding Corp[oral] is a bloody [sight] worse than our old Sgt O'Brien. The way he yells!' Standing outside the Orderly Room [was] his Company Sgt. Major (the same one that farewelled him some months ago), and, in a very sarcastic voice [he said] 'Well, well, so the little Cockney boy tried to run away, and Your Commander will not be very pleased with your desertion.'

'Gor blimey, Sgt. Major, I didn't desert!'

'Silence!', he roared, 'Don't answer back and don't speak till I give you permission!'

The Sgt. gave the order, 'Escort and prisoner, left turn, quick March, left, right and son, left turn, Cap off!'

It was a different [Captain] to the one that sentenced him some weeks ago. The Sgt. (the swagger stick under his arm) [said] in his parade voice, 'Sir! No. 17787, Pte. Edward Casey is charged with being Absent without leave till being arrested by Military police in Dublin.'

I kind of like[d] this Captain — he did not get angry like the other bloke. In a kindly, soft voice, [he] said, 'Well, Casey, have you anything to say in defence?'

'Well, sir, The Sgt. Major frightened the bells out of me when he yelled, "Prisoner, stand at attention!" Oh no, Sir, only that I kinda liked Dublin and enjoyed it so much so I stayed a few days extra.'

He replied, 'Well, I do hope you enjoyed it because I'm going to confine you to Camp [...] for 28 days. You are also fined 14 days pay.'

'Oh Christ!, Gov!, I mean, Sir! I'm broke now, and 28 days without pay is a bit stiff!'

'Silence!' yelled the Sgt. Major.

Smiling, the Captain said, 'Take him away. See his training continues: he is marked A1 now and fit for active service.'

This savage sentence upset me and I almost cried with rage. The next 28 days went by and I was a very bitter and angry [man]. He was thinking what he was going to do, and how he was going to do it. He (with many [others] on yankers) were pushed around by Sgts., Corporals, and even the bloody Lance jaks had a piece of me, and Christ knows how many more. Many Others were waiting to give me orders and jobs. Every time the Defaulter's bugle blew, I had to run like hell to the Guard Room, where his Majesty, the bleedin', bloody Son of a Whore (the Orderly Sgt.) was waiting to give us orders.

[*He describes the chores and training.* Circa 1,790 words]

And so the training went on day after day. Then going into the City in the evening, was now very boring. In my early days (before going to France) you did get a smile from the locals. Nowadays it was different. We were told the Sein Fein movement were getting stronger every week. There was no violence, and when the folks saw a Soldier they would cross to the other side of the street. And if a group went to a pub to have a pint of porter, the men drinking at the bar would move. Nobody spoke, or even nodded their heads. To me, it was a very chilling experience, and in my own little mind, [I] saw great trouble and bloodshed ahead. Sometimes on Sundays (after Church parade) I managed to borrow a Company [bicycle] from the Scout training Sgt. I was able to visit [some] of the people I knew before, but this time I was not welcome and was told [that] if I did not want to get them into trouble, please keep away from us. And [so] it was with a sad heart [that] I continued my pedaling. I often sought out the Parish Priest, and enjoyed the talks I had with him. I ask[ed him] why did his flock, who were friendly before, change now? [The priest replied] 'My Son, the Rebels are very strong in the District now. It is forbidden to talk or give succour to the enemy.'

[I said] 'If their hatred is so bitter, as you say, why do they go to England? You [know] Father, there are thousands of Irishmen working in England. My Dad is one. And I know he wants home rule for Ireland, [but] he is not rabid and bitter.'

[The priest said] 'Remember, my Son, beggars cannot be choosers. These people have little or no money for fares to England. If they had, they would leave in droves. The Rebels are few in numbers but strong in persuasion. My people are terrified at the approach of the Rebels. So I do advise you not to ride your cycle in these parts. It could be stolen. You know they are stealing rifles and ammunition, and other military equipment they can get [or] lay their [hands upon] or [they] buy [them] from Troops who sympathize with the movement.'

[I said] 'I am very sorry to hear such bad news, and although I am not so patriotic as I was when I joined, I cannot condone their actions. By being at war with us when we are at war with Germany [they are stabbing us in the back].'

[The priest said] 'You must understand, my Son, an Irishman will fight with anyone or anybody. He is always agin any Government, and when the day comes, he will be agin his own Government.'

The reinforcement draft were given the seven days final leave. [I was told] 'Now don't go adrift this time, will you Casey?' He was also warned not to talk about his training, especially him being a trained bomb-thrower. And his Sgt. told him to remember the little rhyme that was on the posters. 'Do you remember it?' 'Never heard of it,' said I. 'Well, it goes like [this]:

> 'A wise old owl, perched in the oak,
> the more he heard the less he spoke,
> the less he spoke the more he heard
> so you be like this old bird.'

When [I was] told not discuss the names of the Regiment[s] stationed in Ireland, [I was then] replying, 'How the hell would I know that? I don't even know how many bleeding troops in my own Company let alone the whole British [army] in Ireland!'

He became friendly with a big Irishman who was a RI Copper.[14] He noticed a rifle was part and parcel of his equipment. Curious, I asked why he toted a gun, [saying] 'Our Coppers in London don't carry guns, only [a] big stick [which] they belt drunks with. One crack and you are down and come with a big lump on your head.' This Copper was well read. He told me some of the history of Ireland: why the people were so bitter and against the British Government. [He told me that] the land was mostly owned by Lords, Earls, Sirs. They collected rents from their Peasants, who if their praties crop failed and they could not pay the rent, the Bailiff (employed by the rich landholder) came with the police and [they] was evicted, and the tenants had to go and live with relations. He also told me the Irish were great breeders, and they and the[ir] children were always hungry. No work meant no food, no money, even no boots. [He said] 'You, Edward, are of Irish descent. All your forbearers were Irish. Your Relations in Limerick, like the local folk here, are in the movement and when the uprising comes (and all the evidence points that way) we will have lots of troubles and, remember, all those Sinn Feiners are not like the Country-folk you have made friends with. They are mostly educated and intellectual people, who love Ireland so much they are prepared to die for their Country, the same as you.'

[I interrupted] 'I ain't going to die for my Country! No sir! I [am] going to make sure I live.'

[I then heard the copper] repeating, 'I am a poor, ignorant Irish Policeman. [I] dread the day the uprising starts. And that day, Casey, will [occur] before this War (which is killing thousands of people, both Civil[ian] and Military) [is over]. France is getting saturated with human blood, and when I read the casualties, it [is] just [as] if only women will be left. Our future is looking very bleak. But like you, Edward, we will have to grin and bear this problem. I don't think like you: I firmly believe we will win this war. It's nearly two years since it started. We have been getting a bloody good hiding, and so are the Jerries. I am very sorry you are to be sent overseas again, [after] what you told me of your terrible experience. I thought they would have graded you A3 and unfit for active service.'

'Not me', said I, 'I feel ok now, and will be lucky. If I don't survive, well san fairy ann, [*cela ne fait rien*] as the French would say.'

[He said] 'If I don't see you again, Edward, god bless and protect you, and remember you are a Roman Catholic. Do your duty to the Church, attend Mass, go to confession and Holy Communion, always carry your Rosary beads, and I give you this medal from St. Francis. Wear it around your neck at all times. When your time comes, you will go straight to heaven.'

In saying goodbye to his copper friend, I felt very elated, happy, and pure, just like I felt after going to confession and doing his penance — till later when he [had] those sinful thoughts and played with himself till he got relief. He always felt disgusted with himself after the act, remembering what the Priest told him: those carnal acts (if continued) will send him blind, and when he got married he would not be able to perform carnally. He would not be able to father children. And in spite of all those dreadful warnings, he continued with his vice.

[*He returns to France, to train at Etapps.* Circa 330 words]

It was at this training camp, I had my second whore. Noticing a long line of Soldiers lined-up outside some huts, and (making enquiries) [I] was told it was the camp brothel. The whores were clean and free from the pox. They were examined by our own Doctors and not allowed if they were found dirty. After the queue moved slowly forward, I was too interested in the movement of the blokes in front, and for the moment he forgot what he was waiting for. When he was almost at the door, he remembered and by this time he was standing in front of the usual old Lady cock-examiner. Opening my fly, pulling out my thing, I noticed her hands were dirty. I must have passed the examination. She held up five fingers and said 'francs'. A young girl came, led me by the hand and to a very small room. The furnishings were unlike any room I had ever seen, even our bedrooms at home. Although they sleep 4 (two to a bed) we still had a few holy pictures and a looking glass and a couple of chairs. But this dirty-looking girl only had a stretcher with a very thin sheet and blanket. My Whore was in a hurry, taking off a kind of slip and (like the other one) lay without any clothes on [and] said, 'Hurry! Others are waiting.' [She said] all this in very broken English. It took me a while to unbutton my tunic, undo my braces, take off my pants and long underpants. I felt a little proud of myself because my member was standing out as stiff as a ramrod. [I felt her] pulling me on top of her, and guiding my stifun [*stiff one*] into her. She began to move her body in a circular motion, and with[out] making a move I ejaculated. I got the shock of my life: I was finished before I had started. Finished, the girl washed my business [and] said, 'You were very quick and very good.' I was hustled out the door and on to the street. The queue was (I thought) longer than when I went [in]. I was told there was about six or seven girls employed to cater for our carnal needs. The Officers and NCOs, had their own Brothels. [When I was] telling my mates I had had my first women, [they asked] 'Oh Casey, what was it like, and did you enjoy it?' [I was] saying, 'It was not as good as I thought. It's a bit like pulling your thing, but you have someone to talk to.' This statement brought a gust of loud laughter from them. The only thing different was I did not feel ashamed of myself.

All good things come to an end because a few nights later we were marching in the dark towards the front line. I was told we [were] at

Ypres. I remember seeing the shelled-out remains of the Cloth Hall.
The routine had not changed: four days in the rest in reserve or at the
rear. The night work of carrying rations etc to the front-line was the
same. It was a few days later our bombing squad went into action. Six
of us (with the Officer and Sgt) crawled over the top, crawling through
the gaps in our wire. It was a very short distance before we came to
Jerrys' wire. Very quietly and lying close to the wire, it was like my
first time, but I could not slither back. I was one of the team. It was our
Officer who led our section. He also cut the wire, giving the signal by
touching. In a flash we threw our bombs in the trench. After they went
off, we quickly fell in the trench. The smell of cordite and blood was
terrible. The Bayonet-man was standing at the entrance of the dugout,
yelling, 'How many are there?' Receiving only shouts, he lobbed a couple of mills[15] down in the darkness, yelling, 'Share this among you!' It
took only minutes to cover several bays when we came to a communication trench. We flung ourselves over the top, waited until the rest of
them appeared, then (led by the Officer) regained our own trenches.
The strain was so great and my fright was so intense, I laid down in the
trench and sobbed. I was thankful I was not seen or heard. Jerrys' guns
opened up and, as we crawled into the dugouts, I lay in the dirt for
some hours till daylight. I got a double ration of rum, and when return-
ing through the communication trench to [the] reserve [trench], I was
half drunk and felt reckless, and would have [gone] if [...] told [to] do
the raid over again.

Back in the billets, reaction set in. I got the shakes. Rolling my blan-
ket around me, I just laid and trembled, tears running down my cheeks.
I was thankful my spasm went not noticed. Later in the day [I was] able
to talk with the others about the raid. Like me, nobody was willing to
repeat the raid again. The bayonet-man showed [how] sick he felt. [He
said] 'I had to finish three of them in the dark. I could not see what I
was [doing]. I could feel the bayonet but getting [it] out [of the bodies]
was difficult: it kind of stuck. No more for me. I am reporting sick.' I
never saw him again. It was then I began to scheme as to how I could
lose my memory again.

After the usual rest in reserve, his Company was ordered to relieve C Company. It meant a fairly long march in full marching order. The road was narrow and windy, [and] the only sound was the rattling of our accoutrements. In the still of the night, without warning, Jerry opened up his barrage. Hearing the whine and thwhoof of the shells, we made a dash for the ditch on the side of the road. We soon were covered with mud. It seemed hours before we fell in, and [we were told] 'Hurry! We are late now.' [But] I laid there in the bottom of the ditch [until] daylight came, but [since] this road was unusable in daylight, I lay through several periods of shelling till darkness fell.

I was discovered by a patrol and stretcher-bearers, who soon had me on the stretcher and [they were] taking me to the CCS (known as the Casualty Clearing Station) which was so full of wounded [men that] all they did to me was to stick a label and carry me down this road. It was dark again. I was put in an ambulance and driven to a Field Hospital where I was washed by an RAMC orderly, given bed-clothes, and put to bed. It seemed hours before any[one] questioned me. Nurses were bustling around. They placed a breakfast on the locker. I just laid and [was] staring at the ceiling. A Nurse came and told me the Doctor would come and examine me shortly: 'So eat your breakfast'. [I was] lying and thinking: 'They knew who I was'. And when the Doctor came to question me, I decided to be normal and remembered what happened. After examining me, [he] told me I was badly Shocked. He would send me to the Base for further tests. In the Ambulance, it was dark and I could hear the shelling and see the flashes. The Base Field Hospital was a tent city. There seemed to be lots and lots of Doctors, Orderlies and Nurses. My examination was very brief. When asked [for my] name and number, I automatically answered. I then realised what I had done, and although I was still trembling, hands shaking, stuttering in my voice, the Doctor said kindly, 'All right, son, you have got a bad state of wind up. It will soon pass.' [I was] marked 'medicine and duty'.

[Later] reporting to his Company, [it was] strange [that] there were no comment on his absence. It was as if he was not missed. After a few days, the fighting was intensified and we made [what] was termed in military jargon a 'strategic withdrawal', and in my language was 'run to the rear like bloody' [...]

[*He describes periods in rest areas and being under attack.* Circa 990 words]

At night, while doing my watch on the fire step, [I thought that] it is strange how your eyes can see in the dark after you have been looking across No Man's Land. I just hated hated standing on that fire-step: you can't speak [or] smoke and your mate at the other end of the Bay was in the same state as you. I had the wind-up all the time, and to make it worse the constant noise of rifle and gun fire always left me in a state of shock. I some[times] could see (and always hear) the rats crawling along the ground, fighting, squealing, and chewing the bodies of [men from both] sides of [the] armies. The constant biting of lice. And when he was relieved, and crawling down to his blankets, sleep was impossible, yet, when he was on watch up there, he could hardly keep his eyes opened. His thoughts were always on the thought, 'Will I survive? What can I do to get out of all this?' He was thinking of his last experience when the shell buried him in the dugout. Would he be lucky this time and not get buried?

[*They carry out another attack and he decides to desert again.* Circa 380 words]

The next day after cleaning and delousing himself, he took a walk, in a direction well away [from the] front. The cobbled roads were very busy with traffic going in both directions. Before dark, I had covered about ten miles. Nobody took the slightest notice of this lone Tommy walking along and alone. [It was] when a battalion of four Companies, marching towards the front [and] a convoy of lorries pulled to the side and let the troops pass, [that] an Officer asked him where he was going, from the seat of his car. I said, 'I don't know.' 'Well young fellow, me lad, we shall soon find out. Jump in!' Before dark, I was handed over to a red cap Lance Jack. Next I was put in the guard room of this Military Police detachment. No-one questioned me. They provided an escort, and he was taken back to his Battalion. He was then [charged] with his AWOL. Giving me a lecture on my foolish action, [an officer] said, 'Casey, I will have to refer you to the Commanding Officer.' Later, I was standing before the OC [Officer Commanding] and the Batt. Sgt. Major read the charge, 'Absent without leave. How do you plead?'

[I said] 'I admit I went for a little walk.'

'Little walk!', roared the Sgt Major, 'ten miles! You were running away! Right Casey, you are sentenced to five days Field Punishment No. One.'[16]

I said to myself, 'That's better than the front.' As usual I was wrong again.

[I was] taken to the barbed wire emplacement that was like the guard room. In the centre was a bell tent, and this is where I was to spend the next five days. They varied the punishment. The first day I was placed on the ground. The guard then got tent pegs, with ropes attached. With two pegs together, they were hammered in[to] the ground [and the ropes tied] around [my] wrists and ankles. I was spread-eagled for one hour in the morning and one at night. After my first day and after the Sgt. of the Guard released me, I was marched to my platoon. [After] picking up my gear, [I] was off to [do] duty at the front for the next 8 days. When [I] return[ed] to rest, I finished the rest of punishment in that wire compound. I was not just confined as a Prisoner: I had to under[go] the punishment as laid down in Kings Rules and Regulations. Twice daily I was subjected to this punishment and, for variation, my wrists were handcuffed to my ankles. I did not mind this variation because my wrists were so skinny and [the] handcuffs so big, [that] I was able (when left alone on the earth-floor of the tent) [...] to slip my wrists free and (when I heard the guard coming) put my wrists back into the cuffs. Lying on the floor of the tent, I started to scheme: 'How the hell can I work my ticket and get out of this bloody war?' He had heard from [one] bloke who wrote that 'Patriotism was a refuge of a Coward.' If that is right, I admit I am a coward: a bloody, bleeding coward, and I want to be a live Coward [rather] than a dead blasted Hero.

For the next four days, while the Company was resting and in between the hours till near dusk, I was able to walk [around] the small enclosure to get a little exercise, and (watch[ing] his mates marching, drilling, [and performing their] rifle exercise) I began to wish I was with them. It's very lonely being a prisoner, all alone [with] nobody to talk to, and (in spite of all this) the four days passed very quickly.

[*His unit returns to the front.* Circa 195 words]

Life went on the same and when our 8 days came to an end [we went] back to where they left from. Our platoon was getting its fair share of the drafts arriving from Cork. [There was] a fair sprinkling of Irishmen, but the majority were English. Conscription was not on in Ireland. I was told the Rebels were getting bolder and bolder every day, and the rising was bound to come.

My chance came for my greatest malingering effort. There was talk of a big push, and the bombardment was raging along the whole front, and our section (Ypres) seem[ed] to get more than its fair share. The village where we lived suffered a long barrage [of] shell fire. Houses tumbled. [There were] great big holes in the ground which were quickly occupied by civvies and troops alike. I was in a very bad shape: it was the worst shelling I had experienced. When it was over [...] I decided I had had enough and lay in the mud with my tunic covering my head. When they found me, after my black[out], the two bearers lifted me and took me to the Clearing Station. The procedure had not changed, but this time I was able see and hear what was going on. On examining me, one of the Bearers was telling the Doctor, saying, 'I don't think he got one. I can see no blood.' The exam[ination] was very brief and [I heard the Doctor] telling [them] to take me away. [They] put the usual label on my tunic, carried [me] out to an ambulance with four other (2 lying and us sitting). It a very rough ride, and I was very thankful [that] I was not wounded. I know I would [have] bled to death like the bloke on the bottom bunk. I was still shivering and shaking with fright, and [with a] lump on my head (how I got it, God knows). [They] carried [me] into a big tent, with stretchers lying on the floor [and] Orderlies, Nurses and Doctors [were] examining Patients, telling [them] where they were to go. My turn came, and I heard [them say], 'Base'.

At the base hospital, I did not have a clue what Base I was in [or] what front I had come from. I heard talk of Loos, Cloth Hall Hill 60. I was still in a state of shock. Now [I was] lying in the bed with clean sheets, clean body, [and] Orderlies that cleaned him. My thoughts were now on whether I can fool the Doctors. The test came in a couple of days and, during those days, I had to be fed [for I was] refusing all food and drink. My night-shirt was like a big long white [robe], only the buttons were on the back instead of the front. It was very embarrassing, lying naked on top of the bed (the Sister had taken my shirt off). I had the usual tests [like the ones] I had the first time. The Doctors were asking me questions while the examination went [on], and to every[thing] they asked, I replied, 'I don't remember.' The Head Doctor said, 'We cannot keep him here. He requires special treatment', [and] saying something like, 'Amnesia. Shell shock.' He wrote on my card, 'Evacuate'.

Later, I was carried to the Hospital Train. It was dark. I woke to the noise of whistles blowing. The noise of seagulls made [me] think I was on a wharf, and very soon [I was] being carried on a very large Hospital Ship. Although I could not see [much, I could see] only the long wards with all beds with their white quilts in a straight line. VADs [Voluntary Aid Detachment nurses] everywhere. It must have been a rough trip, the way she rolled from side to side, and up and down. Sleepily, I noticed we were in calm water. And when we were unloaded and I was in the Hospital, I heard them say we were in the Infirmary in Bristol.

It was not very long [before] I was wondering, 'how the hell I was to get memory back'. [For a] week or so I was in my coma, being fed, taken to the toilet, being examined by various Doctors, one who (when I [was] taken to his office) [was] telling me to lay down. He was going to put me to sleep. I was telling myself, 'Oh no you don't! I won't let you!' [I saw the Doctor] taking out a gold watch, swinging it by the chain, saying, 'You are now very sleepy. Just raise your arm.' I was telling myself, 'I won't raise my arm!', but I could not stop my arm rising, till it was straight and rigid. I felt very angry with myself for obeying his commands. Now this happened in 1916, and mermerism[17] was then (I'm told) a medical rarity and not very often practised. Those Medical Blokes tell you nothing, for when they carried [out] all their tests, and found I was malingering, I felt certain I would be for the firing squad: it would be 'fini'. The solution came that night. The sound of anti-aircraft guns thundered in the still night, flashes were everywhere in the sky, [and I found myself] jumping out of bed, yelling at the top of his voice, 'Lay down! Dig your face in the mud! They'll be over after this!' [I was] running to the toilet [and] jumping into the bath. I was getting expert at putting on a shivering fit. I heard the nurse running after me, followed by a couple of Convalescents, who lifted me out and carried me back to bed. Later, the MO [medical officer] came to see me, giving me some dope saying, 'This will [help you] sleep for a while.' The Nurse [who was] stroking my head, said, 'When you wake tomorrow, everything will [be] all right. Sleep now, Dear.' This very young VAD treated me as if I were a child. Now I had obtained my objective, and was back in blighty, things looked so different.

The Doctor who put me to sleep examined me again. I had to tell him everything I remembered before the barrage. [Here I was] talking and telling him lies, while he wrote every word I spoke in a book, telling me my complaint of shattered nerves was becoming very prevalent among fighting troops. [He said] 'You may suffer further attacks if frightened or [on] hearing sudden explosions. All you require now (for a while) is rest, exercise, and good food.'

After my usual 7 days leave, it felt strange to get into Khaki after the hospital blues. On his discharge he was given two gold stripes and was told to put them on his sleeve. They were to show that you are a wounded Soldier. I liked Bristol — it was a very nice city with lots of ships coming and going. The Bristol was a very busy waterway with coal ships from Cardiff.

Reporting back to his Battalion in Cork, it was as if he had never left the Barracks. [He was] excused drills and training. His old enemy, the Warder Sgt, had retired on pension. His replacement was a little more human. He seemed to take a fancy to me and gave me the easy jobs, including the Orderly Man's duties. I did not smoke a lot, nor was I over-fond of the black beer. It was only when he was in company in the wet Canteen, telling tall-tales to Recruits of his experiences at the front [that he would drink]. I used to love that — telling all the lies I could think of, drinking their beer [which] they paid for. But still I went back to my old love when I got my pay: that was, the pint mug of tea, a large rock bun, and a big bar of Fry's chocolate cream. Those were happy days, and for the first time for a very long time he loved his life in the Army. His Platoon treated him with respect. Most of them were conscripts from Liverpool, and they were all Retired Christians — my little joke again, Roman Catholics.

Their training was almost finished. We were talking and the bugle blew [for] the Assembly. Rushing to the Barrack Square, it took a while for them be assembled in fours, and numbered, and the Batt SM [Battalion Sergeant Major] (the same old Bastard which delighted to see me in trouble) [was] calling us to attention. Our Commander addressed us, telling us our Easter was cancelled, and that trouble had broken out in Dublin,[18] and a special [train] was being prepared, and we would leave in full marching order, and Live ammo [*ammunition*] will be issued. Dismiss. The order was calmly received. There was no panic. The packing for the full marching did not take long (it was always ready for night operations training). Later, marching down the hill to the Station, we saw little or no folks on the streets. The special train was waiting. We detrained at Dublin in a few hours, [when] it was just getting daylight.

Marching in columns of fours, we were told by our Officers, 'This is not war: it's rebellion.' Our Company were detailed to cover the Four Courts (this was the Justice Dept for Ireland). It was not long before every post was manned by troops. My post was lying down behind a iron Urinal on the banks of the Liffy, and right opposite [the] Guinness Brewery. Streets were deserted, although on the way from the Station the crowds of men and women greeted us with raised fists and curses. I noticed a dead horse and a tram car pushed over on its side. [We] were visited by our Officers and no word was spoken. The day dragged on. We were relieved every two hours and marched to Victoria Barracks for meals. It was two [hours] on, two off. I was standing behind my iron box when I noticed an old Lady walking slowly along the street. When she was in hearing distance, I yelled, 'Halt! who goes there!' 'Oh Jesus, Mary and Joseph!', came the reply. It was amusing, but to me very sad. That old lady with her Irish accent reminded me so much of my Mother. Leading her by the arm to the shelter of urinal, I told her she may have to stay a while. Shots were being fired now and again from the big concrete building across the road. I watched the surrender of the Rebels, Countess Mackovish, [*Markievicz*] and a foreigner called De Valera, and a lot of others.[19] They had surrendered and [were] taken under escort to Mount Joy prison, and with that short respite it seemed the short rebellion was over. [After] a few days on duty patrolling the streets, we were marched out, entrained for Cork and [sent] back to duty.

I was told [that] as I had not taken my Easter leave, I would be granted 7 days, so it was back to London. On the train from Fishguard I was sharing a carriage with Englishmen who were going on final leave. It was easy to see that all those Tommys who had (like me) joined Irish Regiments were upset at the rising. We discussed the matter [with] those blokes [in] the Munster Fus[iliers], Connaught Rangers, and a few Kings Royal Irish Rifles.

Arriving in London, it did not take long to get to Tidal Basin [Station] and no 26, Kerry Street. He (as usual) was short of money and had a quiet time (for a few days), saying goodbye with the usual parting ('see you in the soup'). I now decided my fighting days were over. I knew the west end [of London] was very dangerous. I knew thousands of deserters were loose. He remembered the raids on the Union Jack Club[20] when he was on leave, early on. I was still broke and [was being] fed at the various stalls around London railway stations. I knew I could not ride the underground without tickets. Busses and trams were in the same boat. So [I was] getting back in my old habit of talking to myself when worried. [I said] 'Casey, you are now about to go back to your old trade as a beggar or a experienced Cadger.' Picking a well dressed bloke, with a rolled brolly, spats, and a bowler, [I said] 'Excuse me, Sir, I am in a little difficulty. Somehow I've lost my money. I want to visit my Mother who lives in Canning Town. Would you be so kind to lend me the money for fares?'

[He replied] 'Certainly my Boy, I can understand your problem. When I was your age, I sometimes lost my money. Be warned, those bad girls think Soldiers are fair game and they rob you right while you are putting your pants on.'

[I stammered] 'You are so understanding, sir.'

[He said] 'Is ten shillings enough to get you home?'

He was adrift for a long while, roaming the streets, letting the queers pick him up [and] giving him money. Even Girls on the game were generous in giving him a few shillings. I had a very narrow escape one night. I was with a very drunken whore, arm in arm, singing. I told her I was broke and adrift. [She said] 'Don't worry darling, come home with me. I have plenty of room in my bed.' We were stopped by a Red Cap patrol. These blokes were mostly enlisted from the Guards Regiments in and around London. They all had rank, even if it was only a Lance Corp[oral]. [One said] 'Having a good time, Soldier? Look after him Sister, won't you?' and [he said] in a softer voice, 'Be careful, Son, and don't catch a dose.' 'Blime! they are human,' my Girl said, 'Those bloody Bastards would pinch their own Mother, but that's the first time I have ever seen them let any Tommy [by] without asking for his pass.' [He found himself] leaving her next morning with a pound note, and [this got him] thinking to himself, 'I am now a bleeding ponce, living on a whore. I think I'll go home.'

I was only home a few days when, in the middle of the night, [there was] a loud knocking at our door. Mum had her street coat on (she had no nightgown). Two policemen walking past her said, 'Mrs Casey, we have come for Edward. He is listed as a Deserter, and they want him back.' [My mother said] 'I suppose you will be drawing more blood money for his capture!' [They replied] 'Now hold your [*illegible*] Mrs Casey, you know we have to do our duty.' They stood over me while I got dressed. I was taken to the Lansdowne Rd Police Station. A few days later, an Escort arrived from Dublin, to take him back to Cork. My Police Captors treated me very well and even gave me a few bob to help

me on my way. Strangely, the Sgt. in charge of this East End Stn. was
an Irishman. He would come into my cell at night and seemed very
interested in my experience in Dublin during the troubles. [He said] 'I
have relations in [the] south of Ireland and the letters they write tell me
[what is happening], as they are in the midst of it. And, seeing the
drilling that's going on and the talk of forming an Irish Army to embar-
rass the English Government and intensify the campaign of Home Rule
for Ireland, mark my words, Edward, the troubles are just starting. My
last words, Edward, is [for you to] keep your word. You have accepted
the King's Shilling and [you must] do your duty as a fighting Man, and
help us to beat the Germans.'

I thought, 'Those are strange words from an Irishman's mouth.' He
must have read my thoughts. He went on, 'I have (like your Father and
Mother) lived and worked in London for over 35 years. I do not con-
sider I owe Ireland my support.'

[*Casey escapes, but is re-arrested. To avoid a lengthy prison term, he agrees to
volunteer for active service in Salonika.* Circa 1,000 words]

Now things looked brighter. A day before marching out I was
released to interview my Platoon Officer who was to be in charge on
the long trip to Salonika. I had been issued with tropical kit. He was in
his quarters. Standing stiffly at attention and looking him over, [I began]
wondering why he had sent for me. Like me, he was very youthful and
had just finished his training at the Military College, Sandhurst. [After]
telling me to stand at ease, [I heard him] saying: 'Casey, I have applied
to have you as my Batman. It has been granted. I have read your service
record and, terrible as it looks, I am going to take a chance. You will
look after me. See that my uniform is always clean and pressed. I will
pay you the normal ten shillings a month.[21] I want your word of hon-
our, that you will settle in your new job. Are you willing?'

[I replied] 'Oh yes Sir!'

Not to be relieved, I arrived in France, [spent] a couple of days in
the transit Camp, then [went] on a very long troop train for the three
days journey to the South of France, Marseilles. I (along with about

four other Officer's Servants), were told the luggage (or guard's) van, was to be our quarters for the trip. On the early morning stops, [I] went to the Engine to make a billy of tea and hot shaving water for my Master. The first day on the train, I was now in my element. I had a very good job, with ten bob a week. As an Officer's Batman, I was like a footman — you know, those blokes that work for the Aristocrats, live in big Mansions, have a bit with the Parlour Maids [and] Lady's Maid. What a life! That's the life I want after this War! Just wait till I tell all the folks in Kerry St. that Casey, regarded as the worst Soldier in the Whole Regiment (if not the whole Flipping Army) [...] was picked for an Officer's Servant [...] I am a Gentleman's-Gentleman. And maybe my Master after the war would give me the job.

After my morning chores (cleaning boots, polishing buttons, etc.) it was the second day, the other blokes were sleeping, and I was leaning against the sliding door, admiring the scenery, when the train gave a terrific jerk. This was the usual starting movement of French trains. The jerk threw me onto the line. Well and truly shaken by the fall, I got to my feet and [began] yelling at the top of my voice and running like hell along the track. Although the line was straight, the train was gathering speed, and soon it was out of sight. I was in the middle of nowhere. [...]

[*He makes his way to Marseilles, where he is promptly arrested for being a deserter. His platoon officer eventually rescues him from the local prison and, since he had been accidentally thrown off the train, no charges are laid.* Circa 960 words]

I had three days in that City of sin. Shops sold very dirty post cards [and] every other place seem[ed] to be a brothel. Passing what seemed to be a large hall, I noticed a crowd of Soldiers (mostly French) looking through what appeared [to be] glasses. You know? You know the machines they had at home, and for a penny you could look through them [...]. This was the same, except the bloke on the door wanted a franc. Being very curious, I paid and looking through [the] peepholes was the most amusing sight I have ever seen. A naked Man, probably a

Soldier, was chasing a Naked Girl on roller skates. Gracefully she glided around the floor the size of a dance hall. There must have been at least 200 […] men laughing their heads off at the antics of this couple. She would pretend to fall, and when her mate was nearly on top of her, she would skim away. One minute this bloke's thing was standing out […] stiff as a ram rod and then in the excitement of the chase, it would go limp and hang down. When the girl thought he had had enough, she allowed him to catch her, but not before she had him limp. In the centre of the Hall, he managed to lay her down. When he was on top, we could see he was waiting for his hard on [and then we saw him] spreading her legs and guiding him into her. In a few minutes it was over. The lights went out, and the buster was [giving] his speel — talking for the next show. Still in funds (my Officer gave me a few bob), I invested in a lotto game, called housie. The board and cards only cost a few pence. When I got back to camp and told my Mates what I had seen, one [Mate] told us it was a different bloke every [time] and a new girl. [I also heard him] saying [that] the Tart he had watched had the biggest tits he had ever seen on a girl. He was serious when he remarked [that] if that tart did the Highland Fling in that Hall, she would give herself two lovely black eyes. And all the Soldier got out of it was a free blow through.

[He describes travelling to Salonika. After disembarking, he describes local customs, prostitutes, and dancing with Greek men. They march into the hills, where his officer suffers severe dysentery. Circa 3,075 words]

Now [the officer] was better, he would start talking about winning a medal. Several times when it was not necessary he would drag me on his patrol with the platoon. No other Servant was forced to go, but being a muggins I had to follow him. They called it a fighting patrol, but [during] the many times I went out with the platoon, we would march about 4 miles in this big, wide no man's land, and only once did we nearly collide with a patrol. We heard and saw shadows in the dark. We were told to lie down [and] fire 5 rounds — rapid — [then] wait for about a few minutes. The Bulgars returned the fire and after a while we got to our feet quietly and strolled back to billets. In my way of thinking, the only things that were shot dead was the wild dogs.

I began to get scared at my Master's way of taking me on patrol — just the two of us, walking in the dark, very quiet, listening for sounds, but hearing nothing. When we rested he would tell me, 'Casey, I must win a medal! For the family's sake.' [I asked] 'What do you have to do to win a medal?' [He replied] 'Well, you go seeking the enemy, and when you find him or his patrol you start shooting. If you manage to capture a prisoner, you'll get a recommendation.' I did not like that and hoped he would never find a fighting patrol, at least, at least when I am not with him.

Thinking of the difference [between] the two fronts: this was a different [war], and your biggest enemy was the disease we had to fight. We never saw our foe. He seemed miles away, but we knew he was there. The Field Hospital on this front was filled with malaria and the other one [dysentery?]. In France, you had the Barrages, machineguns, and the lockjaw [tetanus]. Many blokes only got a slight flesh wound and the next [thing] you hear was he was dead with the lockjaw.

The patrols went on and the dogs became quite a joke. I was teased by my mates [that] the next time My Master took me out to fight dogs [I should] take some nice meaty bones with me. Then the dogs would eat the bones and not me. 'Where the bloody hell am I [to] pick up bones?', [I asked]. 'Try the cemetary, plenty of bone there', [they replied]. Then I knew they were having [a joke].

One other episode that went the rounds of the Division: it was told a fighting patrol of the Connaught Rangers [...] found what they were not looking for — a large fighting patrol of Bulgarians who (the rumour had it) surrendered to the patrol after a few shots were fired. And they had to bring them [in] as prisoners of war, and what made the Rangers mad was [this]: the Army gave the prisoners their rations — to teach them not to bother with prisoners again! They retaliated by bombing their Quarters store and pinching the rations. True or false?

[*He is sent to town to buy stores but (on the way to a brothel) is caught in an air-raid.* Circa 240 words]

Before I could make the red light area, the air raid sirens were blaring their warning. Everybody (troops and Civvies) were running for shelter, me included. I never heard the bomb explode. The blast threw me in the gutter and (like my first experience) I woke to find myself lying in a long barrack room, [with] no Nurses, only male RAMC. It took a long time to realize just where I was. [I was] thinking while pretending [to be] asleep: 'Should I do my loss of memory trick?' [And was] saying to myself, 'Third [time] Unlucky. They may take a tumble I am putting it on.' I did not want to go back up the [line] and go patrolling with my mad Officer. My conscience was telling me, 'Go on, risk it!' Luckily my conscience was right, and when the questions started, [my] reply was, 'I don't [know].'

I lay on the bed being fed, [with the orderlies] taking me to the Lav[atory]. But those orderlies in their way thought I was trying to worket [i.e. 'work his ticket' or malinger], but I just stared blankly at them. A few days later, 1 Doctor allowed me to get up, saying 'Let him stand or sit at the door of the ward and maybe the traffic of men and other things will bring him back to normal.' I was sitting by the door and listening to other patients, and came to the conclusion [that] I was not in a Field Hospital. I was in — and this Hut was — a mental ward. All the blokes were going mad. [I began] watching [the] narrow road between the huts. A small truck came slowly along and (not knowing why I did such a mad action) I stood up and then let the rubber tyres run over my foot. It caused pandemonium among the Orderlies, who rushed me inside, put me in bed, examining my foot, telling one another how lucky it did little or no harm, just braised the skin. Then I thought, 'This was a good time (after the shock) to get my memory back.' My first words after the exam[ination] was, 'My foot hurts.' 'Blime!', said one of them, 'That [is] the first word he has spoken.' Further conversation convinced them I had my memory back. I then told them my name and number [and] my Regiment (they knew all that and they were aware I was on three days furlough and the officer's Mess would be awaiting my return with the rations). [They told me] 'You'll not be going back there any more, so don't worry, just relax and rest.'

[*He is sent to the Navy Hospital in Malta and treated.* Circa 800 words]

It was some time before I was allowed to go out of the Hospital and I envied the blokes all dressed neatly in the Hospital Blues every afternoon [that] we were allowed out. The hospital had two Church Parades, RC and C of E. The Priest was an Irishman and, by his brogue, he must have [come] straight from the peat bogs of Southern Ireland. He was a very nice bloke. I got friendly with him. When his Bishop informed him he was to join the Armed Forces as Chaplain, his Parish was in the East End of London (in Stratford). He knew Father Malarky, very well. From the East End, he was send to the West End. The people who live in that Parish were very rich people and seemed to be well endowed with Wealth. Their morals were very low. Not many Catholics would act as if the war was the time to make as much money as possible. [The priest told me] 'When you [are] allowed on Leave [...], you must visit the churches. They are beautiful.' [I asked him] 'Was your Church large or small, Father?' The priest was very amused at this simple little soldier, judging [him] by his accent, his way of talking and ignoran[ce] and all. The local Maltese were very religious and most attended Mass every day. Casey asked: could he attend Mass at one of the Churches? He was told, 'I will try and arrange an early leave for him.'

I was also warned about some of the Girls. [The priest said] 'What I mean Casey, is the bad Girls. There are many good Girls you will be able to meet. There is a very bad street, called the Rag. Don't go there. It is a street of bad houses. It seemed that day and night it is filled with sailors, Soldiers, and others. These Girls tempt you to do bad things. It is called adultery.'

[He was] thinking to himself, 'Blimy! I've never heard a blough thru [*blow through*] [called by] that name!'

The priest was] speaking on, saying: 'If you are ever tempted, my Son, you must go to confession as soon as you have completed this act. It saddens me, when I see Irish and Catholic boys weakening their young bodies [and] risking venereal disease. Do you know what this disease does to your body?'

'Never heard of it,' [I said].

'Well', said the Father, 'what you don't know, won't hurt. You appear to be a very good Catholic Boy. I do hope you do not use swear words. Becomes a habit.'

The long looked-for day came at last and, looking very smart in his blues (along with a couple of hundred others) [he went on leave]. There was only one drawback: he must not go on leave alone, for a while (till he had settled down). [He was told] 'And remember, Casey, this is an island, so don't think of running away. There is no place to run to!' With a few of his mates, they set off. It was just a short walk to the red light district, and it was the first place [he went. It was] a short walk to this so called Rag. It was a very narrow street, with a fairly high concrete wall facing the houses (that were on one side of the road only). The houses reminded him of Kerry Street, only they were much smaller. I (with many others) stood by the wall and look[ed] down at the women, who [were] leaning out of windows in various stage of undress. They wore no drawers. When they saw you looking, they would raise their skirts [and] expose their thing's hair, and almost [all] of them had very flabby tits — big but droopy. Hanging down, they did not look very nice. In spite of [their] looks, [he] felt that sinful feeling coming on and was glad when the crowd [he] was with moved along [to where] the taverns were busy selling pints of beer. That part [of town] reminded me of London. The names of the pubs were the same: king's head, boar's head, duke's head. We crowded in, ordering pints. Each pint glass cost tuppence. [He] could only drink one pint. He excused himself and told his mates he would [wait] at the wall in the Rag. Going back to the wall, [he] loved watching them whores. They were interesting. [They were] still looking out of the windows, preening themselves, making loving gestures, speaking [about] how good they were in bed, and very cheap. The ones in the windows reminded him of pictures without any glass. The only difference [was that] they were moving. [After] looking more closely [at them] [...] he decided to walk down the street. Some seemed very young. I was told they went on the game at the average [age] of 14 and after about five years they looked like old women. His mates found him and all were half drunk [and they kept] telling him they were very horny. [They] started looking at the girls. They wanted to [make] love. In spite of their efforts to lure him in[to] one of the house (even offering to pay his fee) [he refused]. A three-penny piece would pay for a short time: if [it was] later in the evening [and] you wanted an all-night session, it cost a shilling. I felt like a ride in bed [and was] shy but willing [but I] resisted them still and promised I would wait for them to have their pleasure. [He couldn't help] listening to his mates talk. He heard one say, 'You know what I think? Casey has never had a bit in his life!' So, back in the ward, they decided to question me. I told them they [were] wrong. He had had a woman in France. They urged me to tell them about it. Did I enjoy it? [Did] she pass any remarks at the sizes of his dicky? How long did it take him to come? I felt very embarrassed at these questions, but they kept on and on and on. [One said] 'I bet it was your first blow through. Was it, Casey?' I knew it was very amusing to them, but to me it was the worst ordeal I had had. [I ended up] saying to them [that] it was 'very sinful to talk about such things. [I] am going to be [going].' [They were] saying, 'Don't go yet, Casey, its still early and when you're allowed to go out alone, we will bet you, [that] you will be going to look for a nice little hole where you can dip you wick.' He asked what they meant: the only wicks he knew was the wicks in candles, and [he] ain't got no bleeding wick. Their [laughter] was so raucous and loud! The male nurse came to find out what all the noise was about. [After] telling [the nurse] what [he] had said, [the nurse] gave a smile and told them not to tease him: 'Don't you think he is a bit too young to feel his oats?' [He was] saying angrily to them: '[I] don't feel oats, I only eat them for breakfast!' [Then], speaking very serious, [he said] 'Our priest here warned me not to have anything to do with those bad girls in the Rag. He even asked me would I like to be his altar boy. [I] told him "no! [There is] too much kneeling".' [It] made his knees sore. And at mass he could sometimes sit on the pew when his legs got stiff with kneeling.

They got tired of teasing him and I was grateful for the break.

[*He describes Malta, courting a Maltese woman, and religious life, before being shipped to a general hospital in Bristol.* Circa 3,500 words]

After a few days [of] examining, I was classified as C3 (the same as usual) and put in the ward for nervous complaints like myself. It was a shocking experience: cases of shell shock, nerves shattered; some in straight-jackets, other walking around [like] zombies. To tell the truth, I was scared stiff. [I] could not sleep, thinking 'Christ! Although [I] am not as sick as they were, if I stayed in here I might [become] like them. Oh Holy Jesus, Mother Mother Mary! please don't let them keep me here and later [on] send me to the mad house!'

The Orderlies and the nurses must have thought I was not the usual sick Tommy, and I was soon roped in to do various chores in the ward. We in this mental were not allowed leave, and [...] visitors were not allowed, not even family. If a bloke was well and allowed visitors, he was conducted to the day-rooms and his attendant stayed near, in case. [I ended up helping] empty the bottles the patients had filled [and] helping the nurse to wash crockery. I had Xrays, and special Doctors in Nerve Cases question[ed] me with silly questions. And they were all of a pattern: giving me blocks of various shapes [and] telling me to [put] them in the holes. I got very cunning. If possible, I did not want to go back to the Regiment [...] so I had to act and take a long time before I found the right hole for the right lump of wood. I was put to sleep and after more questions (when asleep) [was] shown pictures of Lions and other wild animals. [They told me]

'Write your name.'
'Regimental number?'
'What year is it?'
'What year were you born?'

'When did the war start?'

[There were] the usual chest exams [and] knee knocks. The Doctor told me I was in fairly good health and was to be transferred to a General ward. 'And later we will send you to a Convalescent Home in the Country for a good long rest', [he told me].

[At the convalescent home] some of the blokes [were] told I had come from the Mental [Ward]. 'Yes', [I] said, 'it was like a bleeding prison even to the bars on the windows.'

[*He is graded as fit for home service, and after spending some time in London, where he begs and picks up 'queers', he is sent for training in Grimsby.* Circa 1,380 words]

Gimsby was a very smelly [town], and I spent a good deal of time [at] the Fisherman's wharf watching those lovely, big, smelly fisher Girls gutting herrings so they could be smoked and become kippers. They were a very good-natured lot, and the crews of the fishing smacks and trawlers were also good natured, and (with the north of England talk), I did enjoy their jokes and the beer they treated me [to while] watching the girls at work. They worked in the open air. [The girls asked me] 'Tell us, Edward, what are the French Girls like?' 'Oh', I replied, 'they are all very good looking, [and they] dress in flash clothes and hats.' 'We all know that, boyo', [the girls said], 'What we don't know [is] what are they like in bed?' That made me blush, and my blushes caused a lot of amusement. 'Did you ever have a bit from them or did you not have the money?', [they teased]. I told them I was not like that. I did not run after Girls. [They said] 'But you like Girls, don't you Edward? Don't you?' [I said] 'Of course I like them, but not to do bad things with them.' One big woman with the biggest chest on her I have ever seen came very close to me, and said 'Come on, ducks, give us a kiss.' [Then], putting her arms around my neck [and] opening her lips wide, [she] gave the best kiss I have ever tasted. Her lips were very soft and wet. [She was] standing very close to me, her hand stroking up and down my fly buttons. I soon got very hard down there. [Then], taking her face away and turning to her Mates who were very amused (while

[I was] feeling embarrassed and a wee bit angry) [...] she said in a very loud voice, 'It works! Feels very small but it does work!' With that, three of them girls got hold of me [and], laying me on the wet floor of their shed, undone my braces, took my pants down to my knees, and rubbed their wet, fishy hands all around my Privates, till I smelt as fishy and as bad as they did. Two of the elder women held me while all the rest came and had a look. The remarks they made are unprintable.

At the Camp I soon became [one] of the misfits. The Sgt. in charge of us was not a bad kind of a bloke. He realize[d that] some of us were sick men but not sick enough to get his ticket. All able-body and fit Soldiers were still being [sent] for Cannon Fodder.

[*He describes never being paid because he owes money to the army.* Circa 165 words]

I got to know the local Parish Priest (who was Irish as usual) and was invited to attend some of the Parish meetings. [Thus I] was able to meet some very nice and attractive Girls, who put me on a great fuss. I was often invited to Sunday teas and met the families. It was mostly working-class people. I did enjoy their plain food (mostly fish [since] rationing was still on and cakes and other sweets and meat was still very scarce in the North of England). I knew it was possible to have a bit with some of the Girls when taking them for walks in the evenings. They loved to kiss and cuddle, but as soon as my hands started to wander, [they would say] 'Oh no, Edward, no bad things!' I do remember one girl: she worked in a shop and was always very nicely dressed. After our walk, [we] stood in the dark porch, and [she] let me play with her titties. They were very small, but nice to play with. I came away with a mess in the fly of my pants. [I was] feeling angry with myself [for] pressing too hard against her, [and I] vowed [that] I would be more careful. I think she understood my predicament, by the way she kissed me goodnight.

My next worry was confession: it was going to be difficult to tell his friendly Priest that he had acted very badly with one of his flock. After confessing, no comment was forthcoming from the Priest, and for his penance [he had to go] 'twice around the racecourse', that is, 20 Hail Marys and two Our Fathers. He felt very much cleaner when he finished my penance. He then decided that he would not attend any more meetings in the Church.

He was telling his mates about what happened. They were always boasting about their conquests with Girls, and [they] told him if he wanted a safe bit of skirt, find a married woman (their men being overseas [they] were just waiting to be served). I was a bit angry with this bloke: only horses get served, not Girls. They were very amused at my comments, and told me: 'Casey, as far as women and girls are concerned, you have to love and leave them, otherwise you will find yourself living on love in one room. And remember that old saying, "when poverty comes in the door, love flies out of the window". So you be very careful. You may find a girl [that] urges you on, and when you try to force them, they cry rape. Then its a case for the Coppers.'

That made me think, I could be one of the unlucky ones. From then on, no more Girls — no matter how much he was tempted.

[*Despite all his misdemeanours, he is promoted to lance-corporal (without pay) in order to replace the post corporal who is sent to the front. He describes courting a widowed woman called Nellie. However, he is arrested for dropping a registered letter and charged with gross neglect of duty. Convinced that he will be imprisoned, he says, 'You know, nobody loves me. Not even Jesus. This Flipping, Bloody, bleeding Army has almost made me lose my Faith in God and Mary and Joseph, and now by my blasphemy, I have committed another Mortal sin!' Because of his medical history, he is merely reduced to the ranks. He then discovers that Nellie has become engaged.* Circa 6,900 words]

The news arrived: the war was over. Everybody in Grimsby Town went mad. Men and women who had worked very long hours in war factories, and collected high wages, let their hair down and for the troops everything was for [free]. Plenty of beer, spirits, and plenty of ladies' legs opened for the pleasure [of] men and themselves. You name it: the troops got it for free. I only heard one complaint. One of my mates told me, 'Those very good-hearted folks in this town gave me every[thing] for free, even to a dose of the clap [gonorrhoea]. When I have to go and pee, it's so painful. Its like pissing fish hooks.'

Discharge in my case did not take very long, and in less than a week [I was] being called to the Company Orderly Room [and ordered] to hand in my kit. It was customary for those Soldiers who joined early in the War [to be] among the first to be discharged. I joined in November 1914, discharged September 1918. It was lovely to be free again.

[*He returns to London, then decides to emigrate. He purchases a discharged seaman's book and is employed as an assistant steward on the* Port Napier. *He describes the trip and how he leaves the ship in Wellington, New Zealand, with two months' wages, totalling £3.* Circa 1,420 words]

A final little joke (which over the years I often retold): I came to this country in 1919 with ten bob and my old demobbed suit. And now, 61 years later, do you know what I am worth today? My old demobbed suit.

Epilogue

It is almost sixty years ago when the events of this tale occurred. The intervening years have been good for me, for an old man, rising in the vicinity of well in excess of his allocated three score years and ten. [When this old man] looks back on his memories of what happened and, in trying to record them, my facts may be a little astray. It is in the nature of things to achieve your ambitions and as the years pass and memories fade, you turn back to your ruminations, and what you thought of for so long is now an established fact. No laurels are expected, and will be given. This task has been a very pleasant interlude to a not very active life. It is now finished. Whether it will gather dust in the archives of some war museum, or will be read with humour [or] contempt (or will some who read it brush [it] aside as the vivid imagination of its author or the fantasies of a senile old man?). If a publisher is found and willing to print (and take the risk of making a book of it) remains in the future.

I am very grateful to a new found friend who, during the period of writing, encouraged me to keep on writing, irrespective of the number of words. Mr. Julian Dicsonle [?] Prestion [was] the fait-accompli. When I implied the manuscript was too long, he replied simply: its history should be recorded. My view [is that] it is not an autobiography (only famous and wealthy well-educated people write such books [and] I am not wealthy nor educated). I would liken this work [to] a documentary enterprise, with a lot of fact, and a little dash of fiction. [Remember] that old adage: truth is stranger than fiction. [This] is applicable in some sections of this document. Trusting it will be treated as such.

When my young son many years ago asked, 'Daddy, what did you do in the Great War?' 'Nothing', I growled, 'You just go on and polish those medals.'

Abbreviations

IWM	Imperial War Museum, London
PRO	Public Record Office, London
WO	War Office

Notes to Introduction

1 Sir Walter Besant, *Shoreditch and the East End* (London, 1908), p. 61.

2 War Office, *Statistics of the Military Effort of the British Empire during the Great War* (London, 1922), p. 643.

3 For a detailed discussion of malingering and shell shock see Joanna Bourke, *Dismembering the Male: Men's Bodies, Britain, and the Great War* (London & Chicago, 1996); eadem, *An Intimate History of Killing: Face-to-Face Killing in Twentieth-Century History* (London & New York, 1999).

4 'Fenian', 'Destruction of Kilmallock RIC Barracks' in *Limerick's Fighting Story, 1916–21. Told by the Men Who Made It* (Tralee, 1950), p. 75.

5 Reginald G. J. Ford, 'Life with the RDF at Basingstoke and Life in Hospital, Egypt', f. 1: IWM, 97/16/1.

6 Capt. J. Lowe (*alias* J. Loder), 'Autobiography', ff. 34–5: IWM, 75/80/1.

7 Roll of Medals: PRO, WO 329/2818, A15; WO 329/1710, 459.

Notes to Narrative

1 That is, 'sixpenny-worth of peak and a halfpenny-worth of cap', or a cap with a large peak and short at the top.

2 This is the first of many times when Casey refers to himself in both the first and third persons.

3 Later in these memoirs he spells the name 'Marlarky'. For the entire time that Casey was at St Margaret's the local priest was Father Thomas Moloney (also spelt 'Maloney' in the local register). According to a church pamphlet, Father Moloney was 'the best-loved priest who ever served this parish … He had a most friendly smile and warm handshake and one could really say of his rather rugged face that it "exuded the milk of human kindness".' See 'Correspondent — Reverend Father Maloney' in the St Margaret's and All Saints' Girls' School register: Local Studies Library, Stratford Reference Library, London Borough of Newham.

4   A devotional exercise commemorating the Incarnation.

5   Kaiser William II (1859–1941) and his heir-apparent William (1882–1951).

6   Horatio Herbert Kitchener (1850–1916), 1st Earl Kitchener of Khartoum, Secretary of State for War.

7   According to the school records, these were Maggie, Catherine, Maurice and Millie.

8   Meaning 'Ourselves', the Sinn Féin movement developed between 1905 and 1908 to campaign for Irish independence. During the First World War it opposed military recruitment and conscription.

9   *Poilu*, signifying shaggy, was the French equivalent of 'Tommy Atkins'.

10   Signals fired from a pistol to illuminate a battlefield.

11   Howitzers were large mounted cannons for high-angle firing of shells at lower velocities than a gun.

12   He is confusing Mary Magdalene with St Veronica.

13   Sir Edward Carson (1854–1935) was the leader of the Irish Unionist Party from 1910 to 1921. Casey is here actually referring to Sir Roger Casement (1864–1916), an Irish republican who in October 1914 travelled to Berlin, where he unsuccessfully tried to raise an Irish Brigade from amongst Irish prisoners of war.

14   Royal Irish Constabulary.

15   Mills bombs are oval hand-grenades.

16   Field Punishment Number One took a number of forms. Generally it consisted of lashing a man to a gun-wheel by his wrists and ankles for an hour at a time in the morning and in the evening. The soldier could not be subjected to this punishment for more than three out of any four consecutive days, nor for more than twenty-one days in total.

17   Casey is confusing mesmerism with hypnosis.

18   On 24 April 1916 a small force of Irish republicans led a rebellion in which they proclaimed an Irish Republic. The rising was confined largely to Dublin. A total of 20,000 troops were used to put down the rising. Sixty-four insurgents were killed, and 103 British servicemen. The rebels surrendered on 1 May.

19   During the rising Countess Constance Markievicz (1868–1927) served as second-in-command to Michael Mallin at the command post in St Stephen's Green. She was sentenced to death for her role, but the sentence was commuted. Eamon de Valera (1882–1975) commanded the 3rd Brigade of the Irish Volunteers at Boland's Mills during the rising. Possibly because of his American birth, his sentence of death was commuted to life imprisonment. In 1919 he became President of Dáil Éireann and (in 1921) President of the Irish Republic.

20   This was a favourite haunt for deserters and black marketeers.

21   This is an error. Casey was actually offered ten shillings a *week*.

Bibliography

Bourke, Joanna, *Dismembering the Male: Men's Bodies, Britain, and the Great War* (London & Chicago, 1996)

——— *An Intimate History of Killing: Face-to-Face Killing in Twentieth-Century History* (London & New York , 1999)

'Fenian', 'Destruction of Kilmallock RIC Barracks' in *Limerick's Fighting Story, 1916–21. Told by the Men Who Made It* (Tralee, 1950)

Fitzpatrick, David, 'Militarism in Ireland, 1900–1922' in Thomas Bartlett and Keith Jeffery (eds), *A Military History of Ireland* (Oxford, 1996), pp. 379–406

Ford, Reginald G. J., 'Life with the RDF at Basingstoke and Life in Hospital, Egypt': IWM, 97/16/1

Lowe, Capt. J. (*alias* J. Loder), 'Autobiography': IWM, 75/80/1

Roworth, John William [Edward Casey], 'The Misfit Soldier: A War Story, 1914–1918', *c.* 1980: IWM, 80/40/1

War Office, *Statistics of the Military Effort of the British Empire during the Great War* (London, 1922)

Winter, Jay, and Baggett, Blaine, *1914–18: The Great War and the Shaping of the 20th Century* (London, 1996)

Wylly, Col. H. C., *Crown and Company: The Historical Records of the 2nd Batt. Royal Dublin Fusiliers, formerly the 1st Bombay European Regiment*, ii: *1911–1922* (Aldershot, 1923)

——— *Neill's 'Blue Caps'*, iii: *1914–1922* (Aldershot, 1923)

Index

Agnes (Edwards' Irish girlfriend), 6, 7,
  21–2, 23–5, 27
  goes to Liverpool, 24
  shaved by Sinn Féiners, 22, 23, 24
Australia, 2, 19, 30

Bristol, 53, 54, 66
British Army
  Irish hostility towards, 8, 20, 22,
    24–5, 26–9, 40, 43–4, 45–6
  oath of allegiance, 17–18
  pay, 19
  punishments, 21, 43, 51–2, 72n
  recruitment for, 14–18
  Royal Army Medical Corps, 17
  training, 18, 19, 20, 23, 43, 45
  see also Royal Dublin Fusiliers

Carson, Sir Edward, 42
Casement, Sir Roger, 72n
Casey, Biddy, 23
Casey, Edward
  birth of, 30–1
  cycling, 20, 24, 27–8, 44
  desertion, 41–3, 50–1, 56–8
  falls off the train in France, 59
  on leave, 37–8, 44
    in Dublin, 40–1
    in Malta, 63–4
  medals awarded, 8–9
  officer's batman, 58–9, 60–1
  resentment of class hierarchies, 1, 4,
    16
  sexual encounters, 31–2, 33–5, 38,
    39, 46–7, 57, 67–8

shell-shock, 36–8, 46, 48–9, 50,
  52–4, 62–3, 66–7
in the trenches, 35–6, 48–50, 52
visits his aunt, 26–7
visits local Irish people, 21, 25
Casey, Ellen (*née* Collins, Edwards'
  mother), 1, 2, 3, 14, 17, 18, 19, 21,
  25, 29, 30, 37, 38, 57
Casey, Joseph (Edwards' father), 1, 2, 3,
  13, 14, 18, 19, 25, 28, 30, 37, 40, 44
Catholic priests' clothes, 21, 26
childbirth, 31
colonialism, 7
Connaught Rangers, 56, 61
conscription, 6, 52
Cork, 18, 19, 20–1, 25, 26, 27, 32, 41,
  52, 54–5, 56, 57
  Edward cycles through countryside
    of, 24, 44
  kissing the blarney stone, 22
  Victoria Barracks, 2, 19, 24, 41

de Valera, Eamon, 56, 73n
Dublin, 8, 29, 40–1, 42, 43, 55, 57, 58
  Four Courts, 55
  Guinness Brewery, 55
  Mountjoy prison, 56

Easter Rising (1916), 6, 7, 8, 55–6, 58
emigration, 7
evictions, 45

Fenian rising of 1867, 6
Fishguard, 18, 19, 56
Ford, Reginald G. J., 8